GLAMORGAN GROUNDS

The Homes of Welsh Cricket

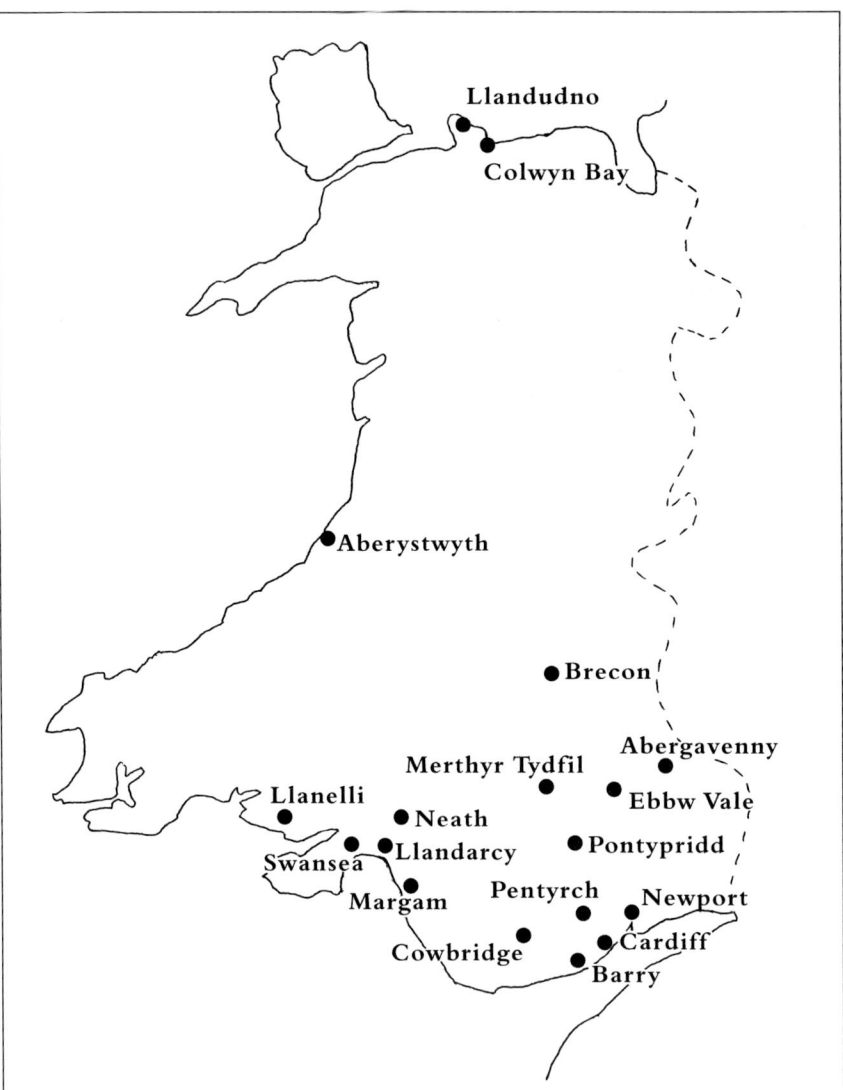

This book focuses on the twenty cricket grounds in the places above that have all staged first-team matches for Glamorgan CCC. The following grounds have only staged Second XI matches or Minor County games, and are therefore not covered in detail in this book – Abercarn; Ammanford; Newbridge Fields, Bridgend; Briton Ferry Steelworks; Briton Ferry Town; Chepstow; Crickhowell; Croesyceiliog; Gorseinon; Llanarth; Llantarnam; Maesteg Town; Milford Haven; Monmouth School; Spytty Park, Newport; Whiteheads Sports Ground, Bassaleg; Panteg; Pontarddulais; Pontymister; British Nylon Spinners Sports Ground, Pontypool; Usk and Ynysygerwn.

Front cover: *Photograph taken during floodlit One Day League match at Sophia Gardens, Cardiff between Glamorgan and Essex. It was the first competitive county match in Wales under floodlights, and resulted in the Glamorgan Dragons defeating the Essex Eagles by 20 runs.*

GLAMORGAN GROUNDS

The Homes of Welsh Cricket

ANDREW HIGNELL

TEMPUS

First published 2002
Copyright © Andrew Hignell, 2002

Tempus Publishing Limited
The Mill, Brimscombe Port,
Stroud, Gloucestershire, GL5 2QG

ISBN 0 7524 2407 6

Typesetting and origination by
Tempus Publishing Limited
Printed in Great Britain by
Midway Colour Print, Wiltshire

J.T.D. Llewelyn – the wealthy industrialist and benefactor who oversaw both the creation of Glamorgan CCC and the development of many grounds as county venues throughout South Wales. This photograph from 1890 shows him in his mayoral robes in Swansea.

CONTENTS

ACKNOWLEDGEMENTS

A number of people have provided valuable information or photographs for this book, and they are (in alphabetical order): Philip Bailey, Edward Bevan, Jeff Bird, John Bounds, Chris Brain, Peter Davies, the late Byron Denning, Patrick Eager, Ches Evans, Howard Evans, Stuart Franklin, the late Gwyn Gratton, Bob Harragan, Joyce Havard, David Herbert, Lawrence Hourahane, Brian Hurst, David Hurst, David Irving, John Jenkins, G.W. Jones, Clive Jones-Davies, Dr R.B. Kemp, Keith Kissack, Mike Leach, Gordon Lewis, Brian Lile, Bob Mole, Hugh Morgan, Frank Olding, Edward Parry, Duncan Pierce, the late Arthur Porter, Hugh Pritchard, Peter Reynolds, Brian Shackleton, Don Shepherd, David Smith, Bill Smith, Bob Thomas, John Vivian-Hughes, Dil Volk, Peter Walker, the late Wilf Wooller and Peter Wynne-Thomas.

Bryn Jones and the staff in the Local Studies Department at Cardiff Central Library have been very helpful, whilst Mike Fatkin and Caryl Watkin of Glamorgan CCC have provided unlimited access to the club's records. Huw John, the county's honorary photographer, kindly helped with photographs, and my thanks to the City of Swansea Archives Department for permission to reproduce the splendid photograph of J.T.D. Llewelyn. Finally, thanks to James Howarth, Kate Wiseman and Rosie Knowles of Tempus for their guidance and encouragement with this project, as well as to my wife Debra for her patience and understanding.

Andrew Hignell
Wells, Somerset
February 2002

N.B. All of the statistics are correct to the start of the 2002 season, and relate to Glamorgan matches staged at these grounds.

The central area of Cardiff, showing the Castle Grounds where exhibition matches were staged in the mid nineteenth century, and in the bottom left-hand corner, the Arms Park where Glamorgan CCC staged their first ever county game in 1889.

1
HISTORICAL OVERVIEW

'Started to serve a county and grew to represent a nation.'

So wrote Jack Morgan, the doyen of Welsh cricket writers, in his review of Glamorgan CCC in the 1967 edition of *Wisden*. Indeed, Glamorgan hold a unique place amongst the eighteen first-class counties, as their name is derived from an old county in South Wales, yet they have staged Championship and one-day cricket throughout the Principality, playing in South, West, Mid, East and North Wales.

This book is a celebration of twenty grounds that the county have used since their formation in 1888, and their subsequent entry into the County Championship in 1921. It also shows how the club have had a long tradition of taking cricket to the people of Wales, drawing on their support and establishing a clear identity as *the* first-class side representing Wales. The book also illustrates how over the past few years, Glamorgan have been actively developing a base at Sophia Gardens, and proudly staging international cricket at their impressive new headquarters, close to the heart of the city centre of Cardiff. This is a far cry indeed from the rural surroundings in which the first games of cricket took place in South Wales during the second half of the eighteenth century. The landed gentry played a key role, and the earliest recorded match in Wales was announced as follows in the *Hereford Journal* in July 1783: 'A match to be played for fifty guineas a side on Monday, August 4th on Court Henry Down near Cross Inn in the county of Carmarthen, between the Gentlemen of the Easy side of the Cothy and those of the West: to play eleven a side. To be on the ground at ten o'clock in the forenoon. An ordinary upon the Down, near Black Moors Inn at two o'clock.'

The person responsible for organising one of the teams was John George Philipps, a member of one of the leading families in west Wales. He lived at Cwmgwili, two miles north-east of Carmarthen, and was the town's mayor as well as the MP for Carmarthen Borough. Educated at Westminster School and Oxford University, he moved in high circles in South Wales and in London. It was no doubt whilst up 'in town' that he witnessed how members of the aristocracy and leading political figures organised suitable forms of recreation during the summer months and, in keeping with his rising legal and political aspirations, he followed suit once back home in Wales.

An extract from a nineteenth century map, showing Court Henry Down – the location of the first cricket match on record in South Wales.

However, it was not just the gentry who were playing cricket in the late eighteenth century, as there are records of cricket being played by the young men living in the towns along the coastal strip of South Wales. During the 1780s, a recreation club had been formed to partake in a variety of ballgames on the sandbanks and beaches of Swansea Bay, with cricketing activity taking place as it does on the beaches of the Caribbean today.

The following notice, which appeared in the *Hereford Journal* for May 1785, gives an indication of their activities: 'Swansea Cricket meeting. Notice is hereby given that according to the last year's resolutions, the sixth day of May next was fixed upon for the first meeting of the season. The gentlemen subscribers are desired to meet at the bathing house early to appoint a steward for that day and a treasurer for the season. Wickets as usual to be pitched at 11 o'clock. '

The limited transport facilities meant that few games took place and, like a modern golf club, most of the activities of these early clubs consisted of members taking part in practice sessions and or holding special challenges amongst themselves. Matches were often held for social reasons, such as the challenge in 1792 between the Gentlemen of Monmouth and the Gentlemen of Grosmont. The challenge was for four casks of ale and a quantity of punch to be paid for by the losers and to be drunk on the ground after the game. There is no record of the result of the game, or what happened afterwards, but one can be fairly sure that everyone had a jolly old time!

In the early nineteenth century, there was a steady rise in the number of clubs in South Wales, and by 1840 there were formal clubs in Swansea, Pontypool, Usk, Cardiff, Newport, Raglan, Maesteg, Carmarthen, Cardigan, Lampeter, Tenby, Merthyr, Abergavenny, Pontypool, Chepstow, Haverfordwest, Monmouth, Pembroke, Llanelly, Bridgend and Cowbridge.

Improvements in the public transport network allowed inter-club contests to be staged on wickets cut out on commons, river meadows or on fields adjacent to public houses, where the players from both teams could go after the contest was over to either drown their sorrows or celebrate their success. Indeed, some matches actually finished early in order for socializing to take place, as happened with the match between Neath and Swansea in 1854 which ended at 5 p.m. so that the Neath players could visit the nearby tavern before heading home.

However, some of these games were still played on ridge and furrow fields, or on surfaces where almost no preparations had been made, with the captain who won the toss having the choice of batting first or deciding where to pitch the stumps. This lack of rolling meant that games and practices often took place on rough and uneven surfaces, and in June 1858 eighteen-year-old Edwin Sanders died of a brain haemorrhage after being hit on the temple while taking part in one of the practices held by Pontypool cricket club. By the early 1850s, the Cardiff and Newport clubs were able to hold their own against English clubs. Officials from these clubs started to look for fresh challenges, and in June 1855 Alex Cuthbertson, a solicitor and former mayor of Neath, organised a

Workingmen playing cricket in a field near Pontyberem in 1913.

three-day match for a Combined XXII of Neath and South Wales against the All-England side. The game took place in a field owned by the Earl of Jersey and the Marquess of Bute, opposite Court Herbert on the road to Neath Abbey.

Although the Welsh side were defeated, this special challenge match fired the imagination of cricket-lovers throughout South Wales and, later that year, the All-England side challenged a XXII of Cardiff and District in the field behind the Cardiff Arms Hotel. The following year, challenge matches were held at Llanelly House and also on a field below Gnoll House in Neath, where the local newspaper was proud to report that 'the outfield was surrounded by a number of refreshment stalls, together with a grandstand for the ladies, a roulette table and a target for rifle shooting.'

In 1859, George Homfray formed a gentleman's side, called 'The South Wales Cricket Club' to represent the region, largely in fixtures outside South Wales, with an annual tour in the London area. By this time, other individuals had organised county teams, but many of these were not true county teams, with rules and annual subscriptions, and instead were elevens selected for one-off challenges. In August 1861, the first proper inter-county match took place at Llanelly Park, between an eleven representing the Carmarthenshire club, organised by Charles Bishop, a member of the MCC living at Dolgarreg, and a Glamorganshire side assembled by J.W.T. O'Donoghue, the captain of Swansea CC and a stalwart of the South Wales CC. Sadly, the weather intervened and as a result the wicket was, in the words of *The Cambrian*, in a 'truly pitiable condition – wherever the ball alighted, there it remained, almost motionless, as if checked or detained by some magnetic force.'

The Carmarthenshire club also organised matches over the next few years with the Breconshire side formed by Old Etonian John Lloyd, and the Monmouthshire side raised by the Hon. F.C. Morgan of Tredegar Park. In 1866, the Carmarthenshire fixture list included an annual game at Merthyr Mawr House, near Bridgend, against a Glamorganshire side raised by John Cole Nicholl, another Old Etonian, and the son of the M.P. for Cardiff. Nicholl had many cricketing friends from both the east and west of the county and, through his actions, a stronger Glamorganshire team was assembled. New team members included the Bancrofts of Swansea and F.E. Stacey of Cardiff CC, who scored 89 for the Gentlemen of England against the Gentlemen of Kent in 1859.

Another prominent member of Nicholl's side was J.T.D. Llewelyn, the cricket-loving squire of Penllegaer, and a prominent member of the Cadoxton side at Neath. Llewelyn was one of the top social and cricketing figures in the region, with a host of contacts throughout South Wales, as well as the west of England and in the London area. He felt that the time was right to form a properly constituted county club to represent Glamorgan. The flourishing industrial centres and ports had given rise to strong feelings of regional and national identity, whilst economic growth had created a number of potential patrons. Llewelyn duly convened a meeting in March 1869 at The Castle Hotel, Neath, at which Glamorganshire County Cricket Club was formed.

The Merthyr Mawr Ground.

Ton Pentre – a typical valley scene.

Whilst cricket was thriving on the coastal plain, there were barriers and restrictions further inland in the valleys. As the photograph above shows, industrial activity and housing took precedence on the flood plains of the river valleys. Ton Pentre was fortunate enough to have a field for recreation, but it was used for all kinds of ball sports, rather being preserved solely for cricket, and it was a place where a good wicket and thriving club could develop. In a few places, a few ambitious participants took to the valley slopes, but as the photograph below of Merthyr shows, playing some ball games, such as hockey, was just about possible, but it was not the type of area in which good games of cricket would be able to flourish.

Girls from Cyfantha Castle School, Merthyr playing hockey on the slopes above the town.

Due to these geographical restrictions, few of Glamorganshire's matches took place away from Cardiff, Swansea or Merthyr Mawr. Merthyr Mawr also staged country house games, and in the second half of the nineteenth century it was this more relaxed form of the cricket that took off, with many of the homes of the gentry staging fixtures against other gentlemen's teams or wandering elevens. Matches were often accompanied by lavish balls or grand dinners, and it was largely social reasons that led to an invitation rather than prowess with bat and ball.

The Third Marquess of Bute, whose family lived at Cardiff Castle, was one of the landed gentlemen to form a team. His Bute Household club, created in 1870, were sufficiently strong by June 1874 to secure a three-day match against the All England Eleven on a specially prepared wicket in the Castle grounds. Several leading members of the Cardiff club augmented the Marquess' team and, in front of a sizeable crowd, they managed to gain a nine-run lead on the first innings before interruptions from rain left the match as a draw.

Some of the patrons of Welsh country house cricket, such as Charles Crompton-Roberts of Drybridge and the Hon. F.C. Morgan of Ruperra Castle, subsequently became active members of the Monmouthshire county club, and these county sides went from strength to strength in the 1870s and 1880s. But as far as the Glamorganshire club was concerned, it was a different story, as no young blood emerged. As the gentlemen all grew old together, the club's activities lapsed, with the gentlemen often preferring to play in a country house game with their cronies, rather than trying to assemble a county side. This irked J.T.D. Llewelyn, who had done so much to form the club in the first place. It was not for the want of decent players, or good wickets, as several potential patrons existed in the thriving ports on the coastal plain. The influx of migrants into settlements like Cardiff had further broadened the pool of players; by June 1888, there was sufficient interest in Cardiff in the newly-formed County Championship that the Great Western Railway actually ran special excursion trains over to Bristol for people to watch Gloucestershire play Lancashire. The success of the Welsh rugby team further fuelled Llewelyn's ambition to see a county team representing South Wales. He gained the support of John Price Jones, the captain and secretary of Cardiff CC, and a leading member of the South Wales CC. He was frustrated by the parochial outlook of some of the

The Angel Hotel in Cardiff with, on the extreme right, the entrance to the Arms Park off Westgate Street.

gentry, and at the 1886 AGM of the South Wales club, he proposed dissolving the club and creating a new Glamorgan side that would select the best players within the region, irrespective of social aspirations. During 1887, Llewelyn gained the support of William Bryant, the secretary of the Swansea club, and in June 1888 he convened a meeting at the Angel Hotel in Cardiff at which Glamorgan CCC was formed. The following year, the side played their inaugural match against Warwickshire at the Arms Park, and for the next few years, they played friendlies against other Welsh and English counties at Cardiff and Swansea. In 1897, Glamorgan were admitted to the Minor County Championship. Largely through the actions of Joseph Brain, a member of the famous brewing family, Glamorgan became a much stronger and more professional outfit, and in 1900 they were joint champions of the Minor County Championship.

Subsequent success in the competition in the early 1900s further boosted Brain's aspirations, and in the years leading up to the First World War, a campaign began for Glamorgan to be elevated to first-class status. A number of fund-raising games were staged at the Arms Park, whilst further decent professionals were hired as the club strengthened their playing reserves. In 1921, these efforts bore fruit as Glamorgan became a first-class county, and in May 1921 they staged their inaugural County Championship match at the Arms Park.

Despite their expanded fixture list and raised status, Glamorgan continued to rent grounds in Cardiff and Swansea, in addition to a small office in Cardiff city centre. The club's lack of success and falling revenue in the 1920s led them to consider playing at other grounds in order to boost support and attract new members. Their list of venues therefore expanded, with the addition of Pontypridd in 1926, followed by Cowbridge, Llanelli, Neath and Newport in the 1930s as Maurice Turnbull and Johnnie Clay led Glamorgan on a gypsy-like existence, playing at a variety of club grounds in South Wales.

After the Second World War, under the leadership of Wilf Wooller, the county started visiting even more grounds, including Ebbw Vale, Margam and Colwyn Bay in North Wales. This nomadic way of life certainly helped to fly the flag for Glamorgan as Wales' only first-class side. However, the lack of a home ground and headquarters also had its disadvantages, in particular the costs of playing at, and equipping, up to eight grounds a year, the cost of renting equipment and seating, and the lack of any winter income from bars, restaurants or conference facilities.

It had, though, been the long-held dream of a succession of Glamorgan captains, from Maurice Turnbull and J.C. Clay to Wilf Wooller and Tony Lewis, that the Welsh county should have a ground of their own. There were many attempts to reach this end, including several in the 1950s and 1960s as work began on the creation of the National Stadium in Cardiff and the conversion of the Arms Park cricket ground into a rugby pitch for Cardiff RFC. The county moved in 1967 a mile or so away to Sophia Gardens, where they continued to rent Cardiff Athletic Club's facilities, and all the plans for the club to own their own ground came to nothing.

Llandudno, Aberystwyth, Llandarcy and Abergavenny were added to the club's list of venues in the 1970s and 1980s as they continued to take cricket to the people of Wales. Everything changed in the 1990s, as the club, fuelled by success in the AXA Equity and Law League in 1993, embarked on a development plan which got the green light on 24 November 1995 when the club formally acquired a new 125-year lease on the Sophia Gardens ground.

Glamorgan have subsequently consolidated fixtures in Cardiff, plus 'festivals' at Swansea and Colwyn Bay, as they have developed Sophia Gardens ground in to their own headquarters, together with an indoor school, nursery and practice facilities, plus new grandstands and seating enclosures. Sophia Gardens has become a Centre of Excellence for cricket in Wales, and a ground at which One-Day Internationals have already been played. Perhaps even Test matches will one day be staged at Cardiff.

2
CARDIFF ARMS PARK

The Arms Park ground occupied the site of a seventeeenth-century townhouse, built for a wealthy family on the western edge of what was the small town of Cardiff. Behind it lay an area of marshland, running down to the east bank of the River Taff. In 1787, the house was sold and converted into the Cardiff Arms Inn, with its name being taken from a shield containing the town's crest that hung above the doorway. The garden behind the house naturally became known as the Cardiff Arms Park.

In 1803, the inn and the Park became the property of the Marquess of Bute, who owned Cardiff Castle and vast tracts of land in the area. The Marquess subsequently developed the extensive docks at the mouth of the Taff, and oversaw the transformation of the market town into a coal metropolis. They also straightened the meanders in the Taff, enlarging the Park to eighteen acres. The changes were designed to allow larger vessels to use the river, but they also improved the drainage, and the Park soon became a popular place for recreation.

A cricket club was formed in Cardiff in 1819, which initially played at a variety of sites on the better drained meadows to the east of the town. During the 1850s, the club expanded their fixture list and played matches on the Arms Park. This early club was very much a gentleman's club, and as the town's population expanded so other teams were formed, with many also using the Arms Park. By the 1860s, there were over twenty teams using the Park, and it became somewhat chaotic with boundaries overlapping, and the serious games played by Cardiff CC taking place alongside more social ones by groups of working people on their free afternoons.

The result was that in 1867, the Bute Estate made an agreement with Cardiff Cricket Club for them to use the eastern part of the Park at a rate of one shilling per annum, and restricted access to the western part of the Park only to *bona fide* clubs. During the late 1860s, the Bute Estate also helped Cardiff CC to erect a pavilion, and given these good facilities as well as the excellent square, the Glamorganshire club staged their first inter-county match at the Arms Park against Monmouthshire in June 1869.

This early Glamorganshire side folded during the late 1870s, but the Arms Park continued to stage a number of exhibition games, including the game in 1880 against a South of England XI, whilst in July 1882 the All England XI challenged the town's cricketers. Cardiff CC also organised a cricket week, inviting leading players from Somerset and Gloucestershire to play at the Arms Park. There was a general consensus that the Cardiff club had good enough facilities and a suitable wicket to stage county cricket, so when Glamorgan CCC was formed in 1888, it was fitting that they should allocate their inaugural fixture the following year to the Cardiff ground against Warwickshire.

Cricket was not the only sport played on the Arms Park. In 1876, Cardiff RFC had been formed and during the winter months, their fixtures took place to the south of the cricket ground. The ground was also used from 1884 by the Welsh international team, whilst tennis courts were opened around the perimeter of the cricket and rugby pitches.

By the turn of the century, the Arms Park was the recreational centre of the booming city of Cardiff, and on several occasions, the Bute Estate refused some quite lucrative offers by organisations wishing to build on the land. Their preference was that the land should be used for healthy recreation, and in the early 1900s they oversaw as series of ground improvements,

A view of Westgate Street in the late nineteenth century, showing the southern part of the Arms Park on the right.

starting in 1904 with the building of a new wooden pavilion in the south-west corner of the ground. It was officially opened during Cardiff CC's match against an XI raised by Dr E.M. Grace and, besides decent changing facilities, the new pavilion included covered seating, a gymnasium in which the burly rugby players could train, as well as a stable block for the groundsman's horse, and an adjoining scoreboard.

In 1921, the Arms Park played host to Glamorgan's inaugural first-class match, which was against Sussex. By this time, the Bute Family were starting to dispose of their property in Cardiff, and in 1922 the rugby and cricket sections of Cardiff Athletic Club approached the Bute Estate about purchasing the Park. They also had the backing of the Welsh Rugby Union and the Cardiff Greyhound Racing Company, and it was not long before an agreement was reached, with the creation of The Cardiff Arms Park Company Limited.

The new organisation acquired the Park for £30,000 on the understanding that the land should be used solely for recreational purposes and was never sold for building. In turn, the cricket section of the Athletic Club acquired a ninety-nine-year lease, at a rental of £200 per annum, with Glamorgan paying rent for the use of the Park for their county games.

The new organisation also made further ground improvements, with the erection of a new double-decker stand in 1934 on the northern side of the rugby pitch. The old pavilion was dismantled, and new changing rooms were incorporated into the North Stand. The scoreboard was moved to the north-east corner of the ground, and in 1937 a new cricket pavilion and tea room was built in the south-east corner of the ground.

During the late 1930s, a block of luxury flats and offices were also built along Westgate Street, replacing the line of tennis courts. This put an end to big-hitting batsmen, such as Cyril Smart being able to hit sixes out of the cricket ground, across Westgate Street and into the windows of the hotels on the far side of the street!

The grand wooden pavilion at the Arms Park, opened in 1904.

GROUND STATISTICS FOR CARDIFF ARMS PARK

First first-class match   *v.* Sussex 18, 19, 20, May 1921

Final first-class match   *v.* Somerset 13, 15, 16, August 1966

Playing Record

	P	W	L	D	Ab
County Championship	208	52	68	87	1
First-class friendlies	36	8	9	19	-

The only limited overs match at the Arms Park was on 22 May 1963 as Glamorgan met Somerset in the Gillette Cup. Glamorgan made 207-8 in their 65 overs with Bernard Hedges scoring 103, and Fred Rumsey taking 4-24. Glamorgan then restricted Somerset to 197, with Jeff Jones returning 3-34 and Brian Langford top-scoring with 56 as Somerset lost by 10 runs.

An aerial view of the Arms Park complex in the 1950s.

FIRST-CLASS BATTING RECORDS AT CARDIFF ARMS PARK

Highest Team Total

By Glamorgan	587-8 dec	*v.* Derbyshire, 1951
Against Glamorgan	541	by Gloucestershire, 1931

Lowest Team Total

By Glamorgan	26	*v.* Lancashire, 1958
Against Glamorgan	40	by Derbyshire, 1946

Highest Individual Score

By Glamorgan	205	M.J.L. Turnbull	*v.* Nottinghamshire, 1932
Against Glamorgan	248*	A. Sandham	for Surrey, 1928

Highest Partnership

By Glamorgan	263	G. Lavis and C.C. Smart for the 4th wkt *v.* Worcs, 1934
Against Glamorgan	273	J. L. Hopwood and E. Tyldesley for the 2nd wkt *v.* Lancs, 1934

The two batsmen who made the highest scores at the Arms Park – Maurice Turnbull (left) and Andy Sandham (right).

The cricket ground at Cardiff Arms Park was never going to win any awards for its beauty following the completion of the rugby ground's North Stand during the 1930s. The photograph on the left shows its imposing, and rather ugly, wall as two batsmen walk to the wicket during the match between an All England XI and Glamorgan in 1948 to celebrate the county winning the Championship.

Further ground improvements took place after the Second World War, following the launch of a 'Seating and Nursery Fund'. This raised sufficient capital for additional seating at the Castle End, new facilities for the scorers and the press, as well as an Indoor School along the top floor of the North Stand. This increased the ground capacity to 15,000, but the cricket ground was still very cramped, hemmed in on one side by the rugby grandstand, and on the other by the tennis courts and bowls green. For some of Glamorgan's matches there was insufficient seating, and visiting captains often agreed to the boundaries being shortened so that spectators could sit on the grass.

The opening ceremony of the 1958 Commonwealth Games in the Arms Park. Cardiff hosted the games, with the athletics events staged at the famous rugby ground. It was a great honour for the Welsh capital city to stage the prestigious event, but during the games, the drainage system in the Arms Park was damaged, whilst the soil was compacted, and within ten years, the Arms Park complex was redeveloped.

The photograph above, looking north, highlights just how cramped the Arms Park site had become by the late 1950s, with the rugby ground, cricket field and tennis courts, as well as the Westgate Street flats on the right, and the River Taff to the left. The upshot was that the groundsmen, such as Jim Pursey seen below rolling the wicket, had to maximise the use of a rather compact square.

Outdoor practice facilities at the Arms Park were initially quite basic, as in the photograph above, with Glamorgan players having a catching practice in the 1920s. The group includes Johnnie Clay (crouching far left), Norman Riches (turning around) and a very young Emrys Davies (far right).

Facilities had improved by the 1950s, with nets being installed using cash raised by the Seating and Nursery Fund. Even so, the county still lagged behind many of the other counties, and badly needed a new home of their own.

FIRST-CLASS BOWLING RECORDS AT CARDIFF ARMS PARK

Best bowling in an innings in first-class cricket

For Glamorgan	9-47	D.J. Shepherd	v. Northamptonshire, 1954
Against Glamorgan	10-40	W. Bestwick	for Derbyshire, 1921

Best bowling in a match in first-class cricket

For Glamorgan	14-153	J.E. McConnon	v. Derbyshire, 1951
Against Glamorgan	14-6	A.V. Bedser	for Surrey, 1956

The two bowlers to record the best bowling figures in an innings at the Arms Park – Don Shepherd (left) and William Bestwick (right).

Alwyn Harris(left) and Jim Pressdee (right) walk off the Arms Park after seeing Glamorgan to a five-wicket win over Yorkshire in the summer of 1963.

The following spring, the ground looked very different, after the River Taff broke its banks and flooded the cricket ground.

For many years, the officials of Glamorgan CCC had aspirations that the ground might stage Test cricket. In the 1930s, it had hosted a Test trial, but by the early 1960s it was clear that the ground would never be a Test venue. Concerns were also increasingly being raised about the ground's drainage. These had first been voiced in 1958 during the Commonwealth Games, when the athletics events were held on the rugby ground, with a running track being laid around the perimeter, and on top of the area used for greyhound racing. Once the Games were over, the rugby ground had to quickly be restored to its previous state, and with the new rugby season only weeks away, the running track was quickly removed. But in their haste, the workmen forgot to fork and break up the subsoil that had been compacted and rolled to provide a firm base for the athletics track.

The net effect of all of this was impaired drainage, and the heavily used rugby ground soon became a muddy quagmire during the damp winters. The poor state of the playing surface soon caused embarrassment to the Welsh Rugby Union who had long treasured the idea of owning their own stadium, and one to match those at Twickenham and Murrayfield.

As the problems increased at the Arms Park in the early 1960s, various schemes were put forward for a Welsh National Rugby Stadium, including one at Bridgend – a convenient mid-point between east and west Wales. However, the prospect of Cardiff losing international matches did not appeal to either the City Council or the Athletic Club so, after much discussion and debate, a scheme was devised whereby the existing rugby ground would be developed into the National Stadium, and used only for major matches. Cardiff RFC would use a new ground alongside, laid out on the existing cricket ground, with the cricket section moving half a mile away to the north to Sophia Gardens. In 1964, the plan for the redevelopment of the Arms Park was given the go-ahead, and work began on creating the new cricket ground at Sophia Gardens. The Glamorgan officials had supported the move, especially as it would solve both the problems of overcrowding, and the damp wickets at the Arms Park caused by the flooding of the Taff. Glamorgan duly played their final game at the Arms Park in mid-August 1966, and after Cardiff CC 's match against Lydney CC on 17 September, the

The Arms Park in late September 1966.

cricket square was ploughed up and work began on creating the new rugby stadium.

There have been no more conventional games of cricket played at this famous venue, although in 1988 a special floodlit game was staged on the Cardiff RFC ground between Glamorgan's side in their Centenary season and the Championship-winning team of 1969. The new Arms Park complex was officially opened in October 1970 with a match between a Welsh XV and the RFU President's XV. The conversion of the cricket ground into a rugby stadium for Cardiff RFC cost an estimated £150,000 and, by the time the National Stadium was eventually completed in 1984, the total cost of the redevelopment for the Welsh Rugby Union was £9.5 million.

The National Stadium had a capacity of 53,000 with 11,000 standing – a vast improvement on the old Arms Park, but by the 1990s it became a different story. The redeveloped stadia at Murrayfield (67,000 capacity) and Twickenham (75,000), plus the creation of the Stade de France in Paris (80,000) prompted the Welsh Rugby Union to consider further improvements, and to create a modern stadium with hospitality suites and catering outlets.

Changes began during the late 1990s, and the work involved rotating the rugby pitch through ninety degrees, demolishing the adjoining Empire Pool and other buildings, and transforming the National Stadium into the multi-purpose Millennium Stadium, with a seating capacity of 72,500, portable pitches and a retractable roof. Subsequent developments will involve the creation of a retail and leisure plaza, with a riverside walk alongside the Taff.

The opening ceremony took place on 26 June 1999 when Wales played the then World Rugby Champions, South Africa. On 6 November 1999, the stadium hosted the final of the 1999 Rugby World Cup, between Australia and France, and it has been subsequently used for the 2001 FA Cup Final, the Worthington Cup and other football play-off matches, as well as other major sporting and musical events.

The National Stadium – seen in 1982 with the Cardiff RFC ground having replaced the cricket field.

24

3
St Helen's, Swansea

The St Helen's ground at Swansea has two unique features – firstly, that it is laid out on a reclaimed sandbank, with soil barely eighteen inches thick, and secondly, that it has hosted international cricket and rugby – both union and league – with the western half of the cricket square doubling up as the in-goal of the rugby pitch.

The ground takes its name from a convent dedicated to Saint Helen, built by Augustinian nuns on the foreshore of Swansea Bay during the Medieval period. During the sixteenth century, the land and the convent passed to the Herbert family, who in turn sold it to Colonel Llewellyn Morgan. By the eighteenth century, Swansea was a thriving port and the Colonel's land adjacent to Swansea Bay became attractive for building development, whilst the foreshore was used for healthy recreation.

Cricket in Swansea dates from the 1780s, and by the early nineteenth century, a thriving club was in existence, playing fixtures against teams from Neath, Llanelly and Merthyr. The club secured the use from Colonel Morgan of part of a field near the former convent, and by the 1860s, Swansea CC had become one of the top sides in South Wales.

Amongst the club's leading members was J.T.D. Llewelyn, an Old Etonian and Oxford-educated industrialist, who had a wide range of sporting contacts in South Wales and London. It was through his connections that Swansea CC secured fixtures against the MCC, as well as exhibition games against the United All England XI in 1866, and an Aboriginal XI from Australia in July 1868. However, the games were marred by the poor nature of the wicket, and in an attempt to improve matters, plans were set in motion for the club to acquire a larger recreation ground which could act as a decent and proper home for the various sporting teams representing Swansea.

In 1872, a successful approach was made to Colonel Morgan regarding his land lining the foreshore. The sandbanks were subsequently levelled, turfed and rolled, and during the summer of 1873, Swansea CC played their first games at their new and permanent home. J.T.D. Llewelyn also helped to finance the building of a pavilion and dressing room for the cricketers and rugby players. In May 1876, the wicket was good enough for a three-day game between a XXII of Swansea and District against a United South of England XI, and in 1878 it hosted a two-day game between the South Wales CC and the Australian tourists.

However, the western expansion of Swansea meant that St Helen's was prime building land, and in 1879 Swansea Town Council agreed to acquire the sports field for building purposes. The leading members of the Cricket and Football club voiced their vehement opposition, whilst Llewelyn offered to donate £500 to preserve the field for recreational pursuits. The strong pressure and Llewelyn's gentle persuasion forced the council to agree that St Helen's should remain as a sports ground.

Glamorgan CCC paid their first visit to Swansea in June 1890 for a match with the MCC, and the ground's first inter-county fixture took place in August 1891 against Devon, although the weather badly interfered with the contest. In the early 1880s, a small groundsman's cottage had been built in the south-west corner of the ground, and it subsequently became the home of the Bancroft family. William and his several sons were all outstanding sportsmen and represented Swansea at cricket and rugby. His son Billy subsequently became the county's first home-grown professional in 1895, in addition to winning 33 Welsh rugby caps, and being one of the leading sportsmen in South Wales in the years leading up to the First World War.

A number of ground improvements took place at St Helen's during the early twentieth century, including a £1,200 donation from J.T.D. Llewelyn for the laying of grass banking around the ground, the construction of decent seating and a perimeter wall. After the First World War, a new cricket pavilion was built on the banking running down from Bryn Road,

A view of Swansea Bay from Town Hill.

with sixty-seven sets of steps leading down to the ground from the new dressing rooms. During the 1920s, a rugby grandstand was erected along the Mumbles Road boundary. By this time, Glamorgan had become a first-class side, and on 28 May 1921, St Helen's staged its first County Championship match as Glamorgan played Leicestershire. The visitors won by 20 runs, and it wasn't until the end of July that Glamorgan were able to celebrate their first victory at Swansea, when they defeated Worcestershire by an innings and 53 runs. Glamorgan victories were few and far between in these early years, but in 1927 Swansea staged one of the county's most dramatic matches, as Jack Mercer and Frank Ryan bowled out Nottinghamshire for 61 to stop the visitors from winning the Championship. Indeed, there are stories of the visiting players sitting in front of the dressing rooms, with tears streaming down their cheeks as they saw the title slip from their grasp.

The two-storey pavilion had been extended during the previous winter. On the lower floors were the changing rooms, umpires' room and a store for the ground staff, whilst on the upper floor there was a bar and a veranda. In 1939, this impressive building became the property of the Swansea Town Corporation as the Cricket and Football Club sold the ground to the town authorities, who have been the owners ever since. The ground was first used for Welsh rugby internationals in December 1882, but by the end of the Second World War, there were doubts over the future of these games at St Helen's. In a bid to retain the fixtures, the Corporation made further ground improvements with the grass banking being replaced by tiered concrete terraces. Further extensions were also made to the pavilion, and in 1964, four 140-foot floodlight pylons were erected for evening rugby matches.

St Helen's shortly before the First World War, with groundsman Billy Bancroft cutting the outfield with a horse-drawn lawnmower.

GROUND STATISTICS FOR ST HELEN'S, SWANSEA

First first-class match   *v*. Leicestershire, 28, 29, 30 May 1921

Most recent first-class match   *v*. Yorkshire, 30, 31 May, 1, 2 June 2001

First limited overs match   *v*. Warwickshire, 21 May 1966

Most recent limited overs match   *v*. Sussex, 3 June 2001

Playing Record

	P	W	L	D	T	Ab/NR
County Championship	327	76	108	141	-	2
First-class friendlies	67	8	21	38	-	-
Gillette/NatWest/C&G	16	7	9		-	-
Benson & Hedges	24	11	13		-	-
Sunday/AXA League	80	39	37		-	4
National League	3	-	2		1	-

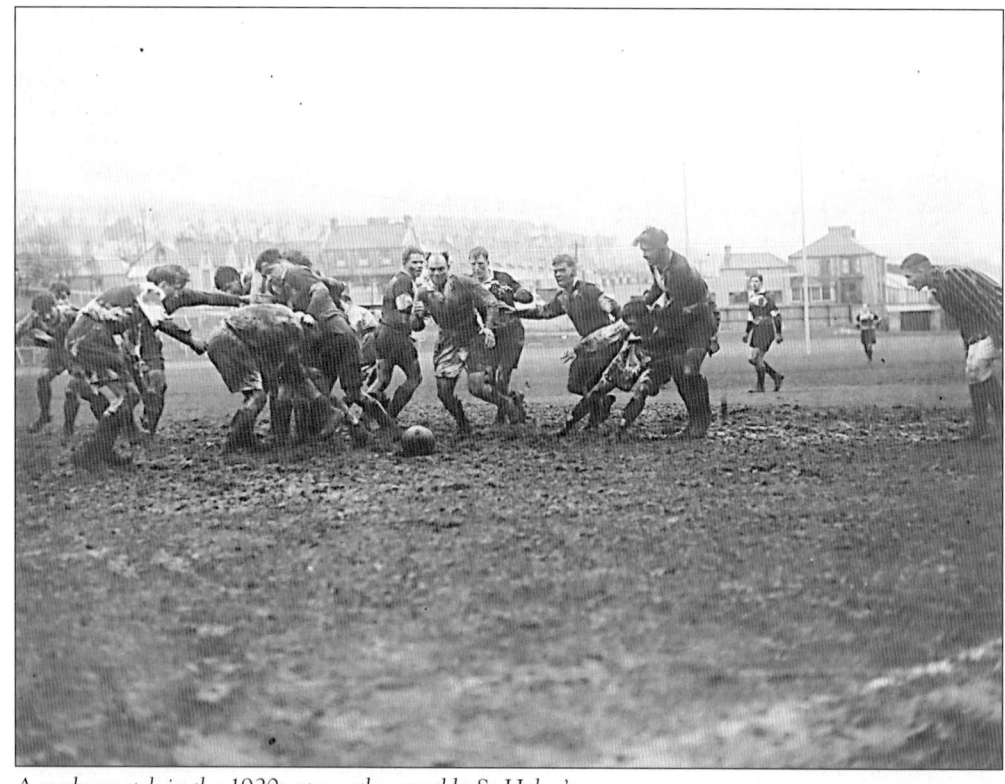

A rugby match in the 1920s at a rather muddy St Helen's.

In 1948, 50,000 people teemed into the Swansea ground for the one-and-a-half day's play with the Australians. Indeed, these tourist games, often staged over the Bank Holiday periods, have seen the ground packed to the rafters, and for the visiting players, their games with Glamorgan have felt like unofficial Test matches against Wales, in front of what seemed like half of the Welsh population!

It was very easy for Glamorgan's supporters to reach the Swansea ground as the railway line to the Mumbles ran alongside the seashore adjacent to St Helen's, and as the photograph below shows, there was a station directly opposite the ground on Oystermouth Road.

FIRST-CLASS BATTING RECORDS AT ST HELEN'S, SWANSEA

Highest Team Total

| By Glamorgan | 547-6 dec | v. Northamptonshire, 1933 |
| Against Glamorgan | 544-4 dec | by West Indians, 1976 |

Lowest Team Total

| By Glamorgan | 36 | v. Hampshire, 1922 |
| Against Glamorgan | 40 | by Somerset, 1968 |

Highest Individual Score

| By Glamorgan | 233 | M.J.L. Turnbull | v. Worcestershire, 1937 |
| Against Glamorgan | 257 | A.H. Bakewell | for Northamptonshire, 1923 |

Highest Partnership

| By Glamorgan | 330 | by R.C. Fredericks and A. Jones for the 1st wkt v. Northants, 1972 |
| Against Glamorgan | 335 | by B.F. Butcher and C.H. Lloyd for the 5th wkt for the West Indians, 1969 |

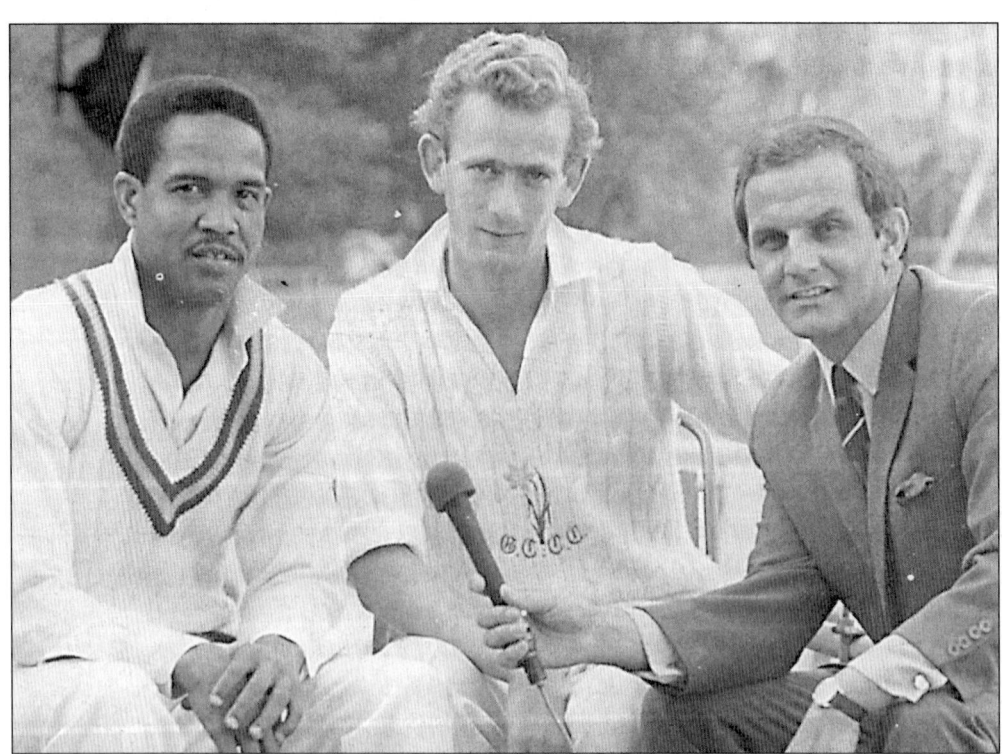

Perhaps the most famous batting record at St Helen's came in 1968 when Garry Sobers hit 6 sixes in an over off Glamorgan's Malcolm Nash during their Championship match with Nottinghamshire. BBC Wales news presenter Brian Hoey is pictured interviewing the West Indian all-rounder and the Glamorgan bowler.

LIMITED OVERS BATTING RECORDS AT ST HELEN'S, SWANSEA

Highest Team Total

| By Glamorgan | 344-5 | *v.* Lincolnshire, 1994 |
| Against | 294-5 | by Hampshire, 1983 |

Lowest Team Total

| By Glamorgan | 42 | *v.* Derbyshire, 1979 |
| Against Glamorgan | 76 | by Minor Counties, 1985 |

Highest Individual Score

| By Glamorgan | 162* | I.V.A. Richards | *v.* Oxfordshire, 1993 |
| Against | 132 | J.J. Whitaker | for Leicestershire, 1984 |

Highest Partnership

| By Glamorgan | 204 | S.P. James and A. Dale for the 2nd wkt *v.* Lincolnshire, 1994 |
| Against Glamorgan | 157 | D.R. Turner and T.E. Jesty for the 3rd wkt for Hampshire, 1977 |

A view of the St Helen's pavilion in 1933 during Glamorgan's match against the West Indian tourists.

BOWLING RECORDS AT ST HELEN'S, SWANSEA

Best bowling in an innings in first-class cricket

| For Glamorgan | 9-43 | J.S. Pressdee | *v.* Yorkshire, 1965 |
| | 9-60 | H. Verity | for Yorkshire, 1930 |

Best bowling in a match in first-class cricket

| For Glamorgan | 17-212 | J. C. Clay | *v.* Worcestershire, 1937 |
| | 15-52 | V. W. C. Jupp | for Northamptonshire, 1925 |

Best bowling in a limited overs match

| For Glamorgan | 7-16 | S.D. Thomas | *v.* Surrey, 1998 |
| Against Glamorgan | 6-26 | A.J. Murphy | for Surrey, 1994 |

Darren Thomas.

Hedley Verity.

The highlight on the Glamorgan calendar was the visit of touring sides to Swansea, usually over the August Bank Holiday weekend. However, their visits were sometimes accompanied by wet weather, as in 1938, and as the photograph above shows, there was a fair amount of room at an overcast Swansea to watch the tourists.

There had been much better weather during the Australians' visit in 1926, and many people swarmed into the ground to watch the famous side.

St Helen's has staged other exciting contests against the tourists. In August 1951, it was the scene of Glamorgan's historic and dramatic victory over the South Africans by 64 runs, with Jim McConnon taking 6-27 as the Springboks collapsed from 54-0 to 83 all out. In August 1964, the Australians were defeated by 36 runs at Swansea, with Jim Pressdee and Don Shepherd fully utilising a slow, turning wicket and thwarting the tourists' attempts to score 268 on the final day. Four years later, 'Shep' was at the helm as the Australians were beaten again, this time by 79 runs, as the Welsh spinners helped Glamorgan become the first county side to defeat Australia on consecutive tours.

Swansea also entered the record books in 1968, as Garry Sobers became the first batsman in world cricket to hit 6 sixes in an over. His record-breaking feats came as Nottinghamshire were moving towards a declaration, and Malcolm Nash, Glamorgan's left-arm seamer, was experimenting with left-arm spin. Sobers' feats were captured by the television cameras of BBC Wales, but they were not present nine years later when Frank Hayes of Lancashire almost repeated the achievement, hitting Nash, who was bowling in his normal style, for 34 in an over.

Many other batsmen have taken advantage of the quite short straight boundaries. In 1976, Clive Lloyd hit an unbeaten 201 in just two hours for the West Indies, whilst in 1985 Glamorgan's Matthew Maynard hit a century on his first-class debut, reaching his hundred with 3 successive straight sixes off Yorkshire's Phil Carrick. The popularity of Glamorgan's tourists games at St Helen's have led to its staging two One Day Internationals. In 1973, England beat New Zealand by 7 wickets in a Prudential Trophy game, with John Snow taking 4-32 and Dennis Amiss making a century. In 1983, the high-scoring World Cup fixture between Pakistan and Sri Lanka was held at Swansea, with Pakistan winning by 50 runs thanks to half-centuries from Mohsin Khan, Zaheer Abbas and Javed Miandad. During the 1980s, Glamorgan also staged several floodlit games against a Rest of the World XI at the Swansea ground. During the last twenty years, Swansea RFC have developed their facilities at St Helen's as considerable extensions have been made to the pavilion, with sponsors boxes and a large VIP lounge. New seating areas have also been added, whilst the steep concrete terraces and the scoreboard on the town side of the ground were demolished during the winter of 1995/96. There is talk of further change and realignments to the rugby pitch, but the one thing that all of these recent and lavish developments cannot change is St Helen's' maritime location and thin sandy soil. The ground may look very different from the days when Billy Bancroft, Harry Creber and George Clements lovingly looked after the square. But the old adage that wickets fall as the tide comes in still rings true, and it is not just the Glamorgan captains of the past such as Wilf Wooller or Maurice Turnbull who consult the tide tables in Swansea Bay before going out to toss!

A packed Swansea for the NatWest Trophy quarter-final contest against Northamptonshire in 1992.

4

YNYSANGHARAD PARK, PONTYPRIDD

Cricket in Pontypridd dates back to 1858, and like many other clubs in these industrial communities, its origin was the result of the influx into the valleys of English-born and educated migrants. A few barriers existed to the development of the game, including the shortage of suitable areas of flat land and long hours of work at the booming iron foundries and steelworks. Consequently, the earliest 'games' were no more than just glorified practice sessions, which gave the labourers and clerks a chance of healthy exercise in the summer months.

Things had improved by May 1870, when a formal club was established, and fixtures were gained with other recently-formed teams from other valley towns. These games were initially staged in the grounds of Gelliwasted House, before a move in 1873 to a more spacious area of farmland owned by Gordon Lenox, the resident director of Brown Lenox, the town's largest ironworks.

The company, who manufactured anchors, chains and cables for the Admiralty, acted as generous philanthropists by giving the cricket club money to buy equipment and also kit, knowing that many of the club's members were men of quite modest means. Lenox also oversaw the laying of a decent wicket in one of the fields at Ynysangharad Farm (loosely translated as Angharad's Isle) alongside the River Taff.

All of this help boosted membership, and in 1897 Pontypridd CC entered the newly-formed Glamorgan Cricket League, playing fixtures with clubs from Treherbert, Treorchy, Merthyr Tydfil, Ferndale and Mountain Ash.

The farmland home of Pontypridd CC was transformed after the First World War, which saw hundreds of soldiers and servicemen from the town losing their lives for King and Country. When the war finally ended, plans were set in motion for the creation of a war memorial for Pontypridd and, in keeping with their role as generous patrons to the town, Brown Lenox offered their farmland at Ynysangharad. Public subscriptions and grants from the Miners' Welfare Fund helped to finance the conversion of the farmland into a spacious park and public recreation ground. The war memorial was opened on August Bank Holiday Monday 1923, and over the next few years a bowling green, rugby pitch, swimming pool, tennis courts and bandstand were added to what became a popular and attractive recreation ground.

During the 1920s, Glamorgan were beset by financial difficulties, and their matches at Cardiff and Swansea saw falling attendances. In the hope of tapping support from the industrial valleys, the committee allocated the Championship match with Derbyshire to Ynysangharad Park. The game ended in a draw following several long interruptions for rain, but despite the poor weather, many people from the industrial communities took the opportunity of visiting the Park to see Glamorgan in action. Consequently, two fixtures were allocated to Pontypridd in both 1927 and 1928.

A view of Pontypridd showing the River Taff to the right, and Ynysangharad Park beyond on the right bank.

Two views of the Ynysangaharad Park complex in the early 1930s. The tree-lined cricket ground, with the bowls green in the foreground adjacent to the river, is clearly visible.

A packed Ynysangharad Park for the visit of Derbyshire in August 1926.

A Pontypridd CC team group from the late 1930s.

Following further decent crowds, 1929 saw county games with Nottinghamshire and Leicestershire, in addition to the match against the touring South Africans. To the delight of the Glamorgan treasurer, a capacity crowd turned up to watch the famous Springboks. Jack Mercer, the thirty-four-year-old seam bowler, did his best to make a game of it, taking 8-60 in the South Africans first innings, but despite Mercer's valiant efforts, the tourists proved far too strong for the Glamorgan side as the Welsh county were beaten by 170 runs. In mid-August, the game with Leicestershire witnessed a remarkable bowling performance from George Geary. The thirty-six year old took all ten wickets in Glamorgan's second innings, as they chased just 84 to win. Fine bowling from Johnnie Clay and Frank Ryan had left the Welsh county what seemed a modest target, but Geary proved unplayable on the variable surface. Earlier in the day, Geary had heard that he had been chosen to play for England in the Fifth Test, and he celebrated by taking 10-18 as Leicestershire secured a remarkable victory by 15 runs. Geary's figures remain the best ever in first-class cricket against Glamorgan.

As Glamorgan took county cricket into Monmouthshire and Carmarthenshire, Pontypridd's allo-cation was reduced in the 1930s to an annual game. Often these games were played on damp surfaces, as the vagaries of the South Wales weather almost conspired against the county club in their attempt to boost membership and interest in the club. It seemed that every time county cricket ventured up the Taff Valley to Ynysangharard Park, the heavens opened, and the games end in rain-affected draws. By the late 1960s, falling attendances and the vagaries of the local weather led to Pontypridd only being allocated a one-day game, but the ground was dropped from the fixture list in 1973 as the club decided to concentrate their games at Cardiff. It eventually returned in 1988, as Glamorgan, in their Centenary Year, revisited many of the grounds where they had played during their history. Thanks to generous sponsorship from local businesses, and the Taff-Ely Borough Council, further one-day games were allocated to Pontypridd. A lucrative sponsorship package, and support from the council, led to Pontypridd staging Glamorgan's match in 1994 with the South Africans, and the fixture in 1996 with the Pakistanis. Further ground improvements also took place during the mid-1990s, with the old single-storey pavilion being replaced by a modern two-storey brick building. In recent years, the ground has staged a National League game, with the match against Surrey in 1999 seeing a superb 155* by Jacques Kallis as Glamorgan demolished a lacklustre Surrey attack.

GROUND STATISTICS FOR PONTYPRIDD

First first-class match   *v.* Derbyshire, 3, 5, 6 July 1926

Final first-class match   *v.* Pakistanis, 29, 30 June, 1 July 1996

First limited overs match   *v.* Essex, 6 September 1970

Final limited overs match   *v.* Surrey, 25 July 1999

Playing Record

	P	W	L	D	T	Ab/NR
County Championship	36	8	10	17		1
First-class friendlies	7	3	2	2		-
Benson & Hedges	1	1	-		-	-
Sunday League	7	2	2		-	3
National League	1	1	-		-	-

FIRST-CLASS BATTING RECORDS AT PONTYPRIDD

Highest Team Total

By Glamorgan   421   *v.* Warwickshire, 1937
Against Glamorgan   461-2 dec by Pakistanis, 1996

Lowest Team Total

By Glamorgan   68   *v.* Leicestershire, 1929
Against Glamorgan   53   by Somerset, 1946

Highest Individual Score

By Glamorgan   150* J.S. Pressdee   *v.* Cambridge University, 1965
Against Glamorgan   219* Saeed Anwar   for Pakistanis, 1996

Highest Partnership

By Glamorgan   175 A.H. Dyson and D.E. Davies for the 1st wkt *v.* Sussex, 1939
Against Glamorgan   362* Saeed Anwar and Inzamam-ul-Haq for the 3rd wkt for Pakistanis, 1996

BOWLING RECORDS AT PONTYPRIDD

Best bowling in an innings in first-class cricket

For Glamorgan	8-60	J. Mercer	v. South Africans, 1929
Against Glamorgan	10-18	G. Geary	for Leicestershire, 1929

Best bowling in a match in first-class cricket

For Glamorgan	14-119	J. Mercer	v. South Africans, 1929
Against Glamorgan	16-96	G. Geary	for Leicestershire, 1929

Best bowling in a limited overs match

For Glamorgan	3-8	S. R. Barwick	v. Lancashire, 1988
Against Glamorgan	4-12	G.I. Burgess	for Somerset, 1972

Jack Mercer – Glamorgan's most successful bowler at Pontypridd.

George Geary, who took all ten Glamorgan wickets in 1929.

LIMITED OVERS BATTING RECORDS AT PONTYPRIDD

Highest Team Total

By Glamorgan	294-4	v. Surrey, 1999
Against Glamorgan	236-9	by Essex, 1995

Lowest Team Total

By Glamorgan	99-7	v. Essex, 1990
Against Glamorgan	283	by Lancashire, 1988

Highest Individual Score

By Glamorgan	155*	J.H. Kallis	v. Surrey, 1999
Against Glamorgan	74*	N.J. Speak	for Durham, 1997

Highest Partnership

By Glamorgan	204	M.P. Maynard and J.H. Kallis for the 3rd wkt v. Surrey, 1999
Against Glamorgan	68	C.C. Lewis and D.L. Maddy for 5th wkt for Leics, 1998

Bernard Hedges, born and bred in Pontypridd, played for Glamorgan between 1950 and 1967. During this time he amassed over 17,000 runs in first-class cricket and in 1963 scored the county's first ever hundred in one-day cricket.

5

CAE WYNDHAM, COWBRIDGE

Cowbridge, a small market town twelve miles west of Cardiff, in the Vale of Glamorgan staged four County Championship matches in 1931 and 1932.

Cricket was first played in Cowbridge during the mid-1890s when E.H. Ebsworth of Llandough Castle decided to lay a wicket in one of his fields, called Cae Wyndham, alongside the main road running through the town. Ebsworth was the archetypal Victorian country gentleman, and his splendid house contained many tokens of his sporting prowess, including a stuffed brown bear, which Ebsworth had shot whilst on a business trip to Russia.

In 1895, Ebsworth led a Cowbridge XI against Bridgend CC in the first game at Cae Wyndham and, quite fittingly, he scored the first run on the new ground. Ebsworth was a very keen follower of the game, and he had many good contacts in the cricket world. Through these, he secured the help of Kent's Alex Hearne when laying out the wicket, and in the early 1900s he employed William Russell as groundsman, a former Middlesex and Norfolk all-rounder who played as a professional with Glamorgan while in South Wales.

As the nearby ports of Barry and Cardiff saw an increase in both trade and population, Cowbridge became a most desirable place for the well-to-do, who were seeking a home away from the smoke, noise and evils of the industrial settlements. By 1906 there were enough gentlemen in Cowbridge for a club called the Cowbridge Wanderers to be formed, together with a tennis and squash club. Initially, these organisations used Cae Wyndham for a modest rent from Ebsworth, but in 1913 they merged to form the Cowbridge and

District Athletic Club, and they purchased Cae Wyndham from Ebsworth. The cricket club continued to expand after the First World War, gaining the support of many prominent families living in the Vale. The Cowbridge ground was a popular venue for games staged by wandering and touring elevens, and with many pleasant public houses and hotels nearby, Cowbridge became a very popular place to play cricket.

The club's members also included many of the area's leading sportsmen. One of these was Johnnie Clay, the Glamorgan amateur, whose family lived in nearby St Hilary. Despite taking over the county captaincy in 1924, Clay continued to play an active role with the Cowbridge club. He needed little invitation to escape from the pressurised world of professional cricket to the more relaxed atmosphere at Cae Wyndham and games with many of his friends from the business and social world of South Wales. Indeed, it was largely as a result of Clay's influence that the Cowbridge ground staged Championship cricket during the early 1930s.

During the early 1930s, the officials of Glamorgan CCC started to look at venues away from Cardiff and Swansea where they could drum up new support and boost the club's rather shaky finances. Cowbridge came under consideration, as many wealthy businessmen, and potential patrons of the county club, lived in the Vale. Maurice Turnbull, the club's captain, and Johnnie Clay, his close friend and right-hand man, had both played at Cae Wyndham and knew about the standard of the wicket. Both believed that it would be suitable for county matches and, as a result, the county committee allocated two county games to Cowbridge in 1931.

The inaugural county fixture took place on 25, 26 and 27 July 1931, with Northamptonshire the opponents. However, rain washed out the first day's play, and the match eventually began midway through the second afternoon. As the sun came out to dry up the ground, the two captains, Vallance Jupp and Maurice Turnbull, got together to see what they could make of the situation. Rather than playing out time for a tame draw, they agreed to declare their first innings at 50, and to then play what in effect would be a one innings match.

The High Street in Cowbridge.

Jupp duly declared the Northants innings at 51-1, before Turnbull followed suit at 51-2, but the Glamorgan side had only batted for an hour, and the Glamorgan captain unwittingly broke Law 54, which stated that in a two-day game the side batting second should bat for at least 100 minutes. Neither of the umpires were aware of this and it was only when the teams and officials were having a close of play drink in the Bear Hotel that a journalist drew their attention to this infringement, and a debate took place over the ethics of the law.

Turnbull believed that he had done nothing wrong, and argued that the public wanted to see a positive outcome in rain-affected games, and that the only way to achieve this was to have freak declarations. To an extent, his actions were vindicated, as on the final morning, Ryan and Clay dismissed Northants for 59, and Glamorgan raced to an 8-wicket win. But the MCC took a dim view of his actions, and both captains and umpires were reprimanded by the MCC for departing from accepted principles. Cowbridge was allocated two matches again in 1932, and both ended up as innings victories for Glamorgan. But Turnbull's joy evaporated again as concern was expressed at the state of the Cowbridge wicket. In both of the games, the wicket started to crumble on the second day, and in the game with Somerset, the visitors were dismissed for just 88 and 40, with Clay returning match figures of 9-47. With decent wickets becoming available at other grounds, the Glamorgan committee decided to take first-class matches away from Cowbridge. Even so, it continued to stage club and ground matches, and other exhibition matches, largely through the enthusiastic actions of 'Tip' Williams, a leading light with the local club and the South Wales Hunts. In 1953, Cae Wyndham played host to Glamorgan's friendly with the Pakistani Eaglets, whilst in 1993 the visitors included the Courage Old England XI.

The two captions involved in the controversial game at Cowbridge in 1931 – Maurice Turnbull (left) and Vallance Jupp.

GROUND STATISTICS AT COWBRIDGE

First first-class match	v. Northamptonshire, 25, 27, 28 July 1931
Final first-class match	v. Somerset, 23, 25, 26 July 1932

Playing Record

	P	W	L	D
County Championship	4	3	-	1

A view of Cowbridge, showing the small market town in the Vale of Glamorgan surrounded by farmland.

FIRST-CLASS BATTING RECORDS AT COWBRIDGE

Highest Team Total

By Glamorgan	338	v. Leicestershire, 1932
Against Glamorgan	173-5 dec	by Essex, 1931

Lowest Team Total

By Glamorgan	89	v. Essex, 1931
Against Glamorgan	40	by Somerset, 1932

Highest Individual Score

By Glamorgan	103	D.E. Davies	v. Leicestershire, 1932
Against Glamorgan	52	L.C. Eastman	for Essex, 1931

Highest Partnership

By Glamorgan	138	D.E. Davies and M.J.L. Turnbull for the 4th wkt v. Leicestershire, 1932
Against Glamorgan	78	L.C. Eastman and D.R. Wilcox for the 2nd wkt for Essex, 1931

Emrys Davies, Glamorgan's only centurion at Cowbridge.

BOWLING RECORDS AT COWBRIDGE

Best bowling in an innings in first-class cricket

| For Glamorgan | 5-22 | J.C. Clay | *v.* Northamptonshire, 1931 |
| Against Glamorgan | 7-100 | G. Geary | for Leicestershire, 1932 |

Best bowling in a match in first-class cricket

| For Glamorgan | 9-47 | J.C. Clay | *v.* Somerset, 1932 |
| Against Glamorgan | 7-100 | G. Geary | for Leicestershire, 1932 |

Johnnie Clay.

6

STRADEY PARK, LLANELLI

Stradey Park is located in what was part of the grounds of Stradey Castle, which had been the home of the Mansel Lewis family since the early seventeenth century. It is known all over the sporting world as the home of 'The Scarlets' – Llanelli RFC, and the legendary 'Sospan Fach' – and derives its name from the Welsh word 'ystrad', meaning broad, level area.

The town's famous sporting complex has also staged 23 championship matches between the 1930s and 1960s, and in more recent years has also been the venue for some of Glamorgan's one-day games. Cricket in Llanelli dates back to 1837, when a club started to play in a field in the centre of the town. By the mid-1850s they were also using the grounds of Llanelli House, and in August 1856 it hosted a three-day game between a XXII from the local area and the All-England Eleven.

In 1872, the Mansel Lewis family provided a permanent home for the town's rugby and cricket club in the grounds of their home on the flat meadowland alongside the River Dulais. The Mansel Lewis family subsequently oversaw the construction of a small pavilion for the use of the cricket club in the northern part of the Park, as well as a grandstand for the rugby ground to the south.

By the 1880s the cricket club had become one of the top sides in West Wales and were able to afford the services of decent professionals. As well as helping to coach the locals, their job was to tend the square, and, as a result, the wicket gained a fine reputation, and all despite having a rugby international played on it.

In January 1887, the Wales *v.* England international was switched from the rugby pitch when it was discovered shortly before kick-off that the turf was frozen. A crowd of 8,000 had turned up, and in an attempt to quell their anger, a last-minute decision was made to use the adjoining cricket ground, which was unfrozen. It was quickly roped off, allowing the crowd to gather around, and the international to go ahead.

Quite what the cricketers thought of this, as the thirty burly rugby players ran and kicked their way over the cricket square, is not on record, but not too much damage was caused as the cricket club continued to go from strength to strength, hiring players of the calibre of Hampshire's E.E. Light, Surrey's G.A. Lohmann and the South African A.E.E. Vogler.

By the late 1880s, Llanelli CC had become a vibrant club, and their success resulted in the creation of a Carmarthenshire side. A side had previously played under the county name, but it was largely a gentleman's side, playing country house fixtures, rather than being a fully-fledged county team. In 1889, C.P. Lewis, the Oxford cricket Blue and former Welsh rugby international, began a campaign to create a county side that might take part in the Minor County Championship. There was sufficient interest, fuelled no doubt by the success of their neighbours Glamorgan, but there was not enough financial support to allow Lewis to organise enough fixtures.

In the early 1900s, Lewis gained the support of Sir J.T.D. Llewelyn, who was always prepared to support Welsh sportsmen. The squire of Penllegaer subsequently persuaded the Welsh Rugby Union to loan Carmarthenshire CCC one hundred pounds in order that they could arrange fixtures to raise both funds and to assess playing talent. 1906 consequently saw the Llanelli ground host matches with Breconshire, Glamorgan and the Gentlemen of Essex.

Decent crowds turned up at Stradey Park for these games, especially for the latter match, in which Charlie McGahey hit 305* as the Essex side rattled up 540-8 dec. before bowling out Carmarthenshire for 177 and 87. A few weeks later the Glamorgan side inflicted another heavy innings defeat on the west Wales side, but these reverses did not dampen the enthusiasm of Lewis and the Carmarthenshire committee, and they approached the MCC

A view of Stradey Park, looking south.

for their elevation into the Minor County Championship.

In 1908, Carmarthenshire were admitted into the competition, but they had a truly torrid time, failing to win a single game in their first two seasons. The abysmal run continued into 1910 as Glamorgan rattled up 531-9 with centuries from Tom Whittington and Charles Elers, before their bowlers ran through some modest batting as Carmarthenshire were beaten by the small matter of an innings and 327 runs.

In July 1910, their losing run came to an end at Stradey Park, as they inflicted an innings defeat on Cornwall, dismissing the visitors for just 29 in their second innings. Buoyed by their success, Carmarthenshire then defeated Dorset by 162 runs at Llanelli in early August, and the following week beat the same opponents in the return match at Poole.

This four-wicket win over Dorset boosted the morale of Lewis and the county committee, and they secured fixtures for 1911. However, their dwindling finances meant that they could not afford to play many professionals, and after another series of heavy defeats, Carmarthenshire withdrew from the Minor County Championship in 1912.

Despite Carmarthenshire's withdrawl from the Minor County Championship, there were many good cricketers in West Wales, and Llanelli continued to be one of the top clubs in the South Wales. After the First World War, and Glamorgan's elevation to first-class status, several Llanelli players started to make a name for themselves with Glamorgan.

The efforts of batsman Dai Davies, all-rounder Emrys Davies, bowler Helm Spencer and wicketkeeper Trevor Every all took place at a time when the county were looking to strengthen their membership and boost their finances. With several Carmarthenshire players in the side, Maurice Turnbull, the Glamorgan secretary, approached the Stradey Park club about staging county cricket at the Llanelli ground. At the same time, Tom Jeffreys, a butcher in the town, drummed up financial support from the local business community, and in 1933 the match with Worcestershire was allocated to the ground.

As *Wisden's* correspondent observed, 'the match against Worcestershire proved a very successful venture, for apart from the win for Glamorgan by an innings, Carmarthenshire folk showed so much appreciation of being given the chance to see first-class cricket that on the first day the attendance exceeded 4,000, whilst gate receipts amounted to exactly £200.'

The Carmarthenshire side, with the Gentlemen of Essex, who they played at Llanelli in 1906.

The success of this fixture led to an annual Championship game being allocated to Stradey Park, and they continued to be well supported. Further ground improvements took place, with a new pavilion being opened in 1939, and after the war, a local brewery gave financial support so that additional seating could be provided.

Glamorgan's games at Stradey Park therefore had the feel of festival matches, with a record 7,500 people watching the second day of the match with Surrey in 1952. One newspaper correspondent even wrote how 'the annual county match is something more than a cricket match. It reminds me of a fair, for the whole town seems to pour in to watch the cricket and enjoy themselves. One might compare it to the music hall, where folk used to eat and drink as they watched the entertainment.' By this time, the ownership of the Stradey ground had changed. During the early 1950s, the Stradey Estate sold the whole of the recreational complex to 'The Llanelli Athletic Association' for £4,000, with the sole purpose of preserving it for recreation. As rows of houses were built around the ground, its future became secure, but in the mid-1960s, Glamorgan opted to take an annual match to Colwyn Bay in North Wales, and to concentrate their Western fixtures at Swansea and Neath. The final County Championship match took place at Stradey Park in 1965, with Essex being the opponents. However, county cricket returned to Llanelli between 1988 and 1993, as Glamorgan took their Sunday League matches to various out-grounds, including the Llanelli ground.

Llanelli CC in 1920 – Dai Davies, who subsequently gave stalwart service to Glamorgan, is the young player sitting in front on the ground.

GROUND STATISTICS FOR LLANELLI

First first-class match   *v.* Worcestershire, 24, 26, 27 June 1933

Last recent first-class match   *v.* Essex, 1, 2, 3 Sept 1965

First limited overs match   *v.* Leicestershire, 28 August 1988

Most recent limited overs match   *v.* Sussex, 11 July 1993

Playing Record

	P	W	L	D	Ab/NR
County Championship	23	10	3	10	-
Sunday League	5	1	4		-

Jeff Jones (left) and his son Simon (right). Dafen-born Jeff was educated in Llanelli, before progressing into the world of county and Test cricket, winning 15 Test caps between 1963 and 1968. During the winter of 2001/02, Simon Jones took a step towards representative cricket by appearing for the E.C.B. Academy in Australia.

FIRST-CLASS BATTING RECORDS AT LLANELLI

Highest Team Total

By Glamorgan	434-6 dec	*v*. Worcestershire, 1933
Against Glamorgan	298	by Sussex, 1951

Lowest Team Total

By Glamorgan	96	*v*. Lancashire, 1949
Against Glamorgan	71	by Worcestershire, 1938

Highest Individual Score

By Glamorgan	161	W.G.A. Parkhouse	*v*. Gloucestershire, 1950
Against Glamorgan	118	P.H. Parfitt	for Middlesex, 1961

Highest Partnership

By Glamorgan	219	W.G.A. Parkhouse and B. Hedges for the 2nd wkt *v*. Warwickshire, 1954
Against Glamorgan	117	R.T. Simpson and J. Hardstaff for the 3rd wkt for Nottinghamshire, 1955

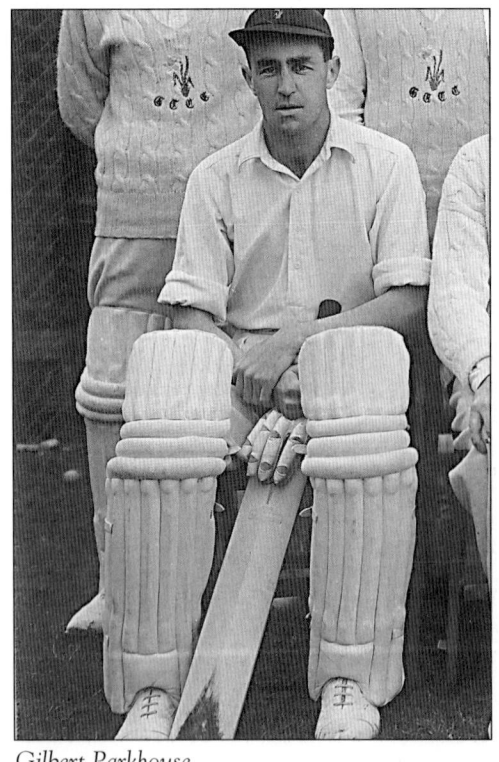

Gilbert Parkhouse.

Reg Simpson.

LIMITED OVERS BATTING RECORDS AT LLANELLI

Highest Team Total

| By Glamorgan | 269-8 | v. Sussex, 1993 |
| Against Glamorgan | 235-3 | by Surrey, 1992 |

Lowest Team Total

| By Glamorgan | 77-7 | v. Leicestershire, 1988 |
| Against Glamorgan | 78-2 | by Leicestershire, 1988 |

Highest Individual Score

| By Glamorgan | 107 | S.P. James v. Sussex, 1993 |
| Against Glamorgan | 113 | A.D. Brown for Surrey, 1992 |

Highest Partnership

By Glamorgan   139   H. Morris and M.P. Maynard for the 2nd wkt v. Surrey, 1992

Against Glamorgan   105   A.D. Brown and G.P. Thorpe for the 2nd wkt for Surrey, 1992

Hugh Morris.   *Matthew Maynard.*

BOWLING RECORDS AT LLANELLI

Best bowling in an innings in first-class cricket

| For Glamorgan | 9-54 | J.C. Clay | v. Northamptonshire, 1931 |
| Against Glamorgan | 8-43 | V.E. Jackson | for Leicestershire, 1956 |

Best bowling in a match in first-class cricket

| For Glamorgan | 15-86 | J.C. Clay | v. Northamptonshire, 1935 |
| Against Glamorgan | 12-94 | R.N.S. Hobbs | for Essex, 1965 |

Best bowling in a limited overs match

| For Glamorgan | 3-38 | A. Dale | v. Sussex, 1993 |
| Against Glamorgan | 3-9 | G.J.F. Ferris | for Leicestershire, 1988 |

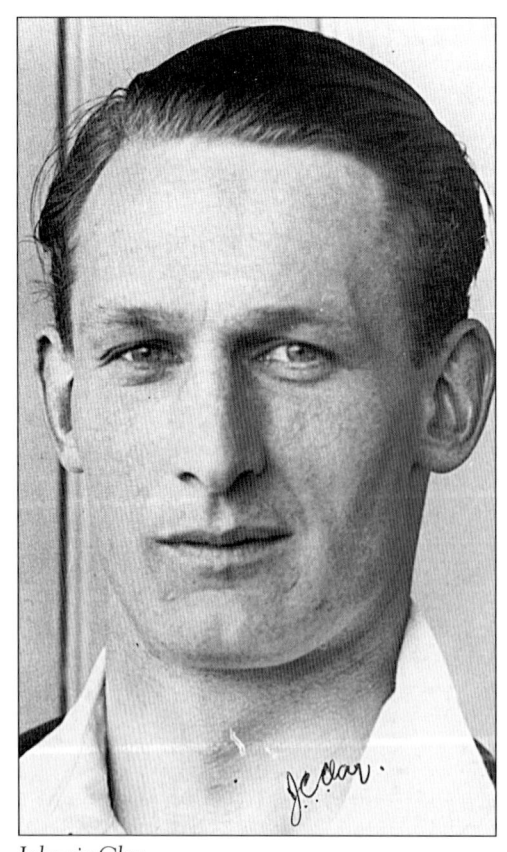

Johnnie Clay.

Robin Hobbs.

7

THE GNOLL, NEATH

Like many of Glamorgan's grounds, The Gnoll is the home to both Neath Rugby and Cricket Club. The name of the ground is believed to be a derivation from the word 'knoll', meaning a small round hill, as the first building in the area was situated on the circular mound on the hill to the north of the town.

By the seventeenth century, a small castle and country house had been built on the hillside, and from 1710 onwards it became the home of the Mackworth family, who were wealthy industrialists and owned the town's copper works. In 1811 the Gnoll Estate was purchased by Henry Grant – the first mayor of the town – and it was Grant who allowed ball games to be played on the meadows below Gnoll House.

The first record of cricket in Neath dates back to the mid-1840s, and in 1848 a cricket club was formed, based at The Gnoll. During the middle of the nineteenth century, more house-building took place on Grant's land, but he refused to sell the cricket field, and the club went from strength to strength. A number of quite prestigious fixtures were held during the next few years as Alex Cuthbertson, a local solicitor, helped to arrange three-day fixtures in 1855 and 1856 between an XI of All-England and a XXII of Neath and District.

However, the club ran into financial problems, and in the early 1860s, they looked like going out of existence, as it seemed they did not have enough cash to pay the annual rent for the use of The Gnoll. The cricket club were thrown a lifeline in 1863 as J.T.D. Llewelyn, the cricket-loving industrialist and sporting benefactor, paid off their debts, and agreed to personally pay for the use of The Gnoll. Llewelyn reformed the club under the name of Cadoxton Cricket Club, with the new side taking its name from a small hamlet to the north of the town. There was, though, nothing small about Llewelyn's ambitions, as Cadoxton CC became the MCC of South Wales. In September 1864, Llewelyn was instrumental in arranging a cricket week which had as its highlight a challenge match between a Glamorganshire XI and a side representing Carmarthenshire.

Llewelyn continued to organise special exhibition games at The Gnoll, and in May 1868 arguably the most famous of these games saw a XXII of Cadoxton challenge the United South of England. W.G. Grace was in the English side, yet, for once in his career, he bagged a pair, dismissed in both innings by George Howitt, Cadoxton's guest professional.

In 1871, Neath RFC was formed and the south-western part of the sports field was devoted to rugby, with cricket being played in the north-eastern half. A rugby grandstand was built and seating was also provided alongside the cricket pavilion as the Cadoxton club continued to be the premier gentleman's side in South Wales, and played with success in the newly-formed South Wales Challenge Cup.

In 1897, the Neath Football Club and Athletic Association took over the affairs of Cadoxton CC, but this proved to be a short-lived organisation, as in 1904 the cricket club re-formed under the name of Gnoll Park CC. However, there were several financial problems, caused by internal friction within the now defunct association. Fortunately, these problems were overcome by the staging of a series of exhibition games on The Gnoll by a side called The Gentlemen of Glamorgan.

The instigator of these games was a young solicitor called Tom Whittington. The son of a Scottish rugby international, Whittington was a fine batsman and he had been one of the rising young stars in Glamorgan's team in the Minor County Championship since the early 1900s. Whittington, as befitted an Oxford-educated gentleman, had all the right contacts in the business, social and cricket world to arrange some decent opposition for the amateur side.

A sketch of the 1868 match at The Gnoll.

58

Whittington also had the support of W.B. Trick, the mayor of Neath, whose brother was mayor of Stoke Newington and an influential supporter of Essex CCC. Through his connections, an all-amateur side travelled to Neath to play Whittington's XI in July 1905. A lavish banquet was also held at The Castle Hotel, and following the success of the match, a return game was arranged for 1906. This time, Whittington secured the services of Walter Brearley, the volatile England fast bowler, who had fallen out with the Lancashire authorities, as well as several top players from the Cardiff club. Several players from Swansea declined the invitation, preferring not to support a venture that might make The Gnoll, rather than St Helen's, the premier venue in the west.

Through Whittington's efforts, Neath's financial problems disappeared, and the club reverted to being known as Neath CC after 1906. The success of these games, and Whittington's bold batting, led to him being elevated in 1908 to the captaincy of the county club. Not surprisingly, Whittington persuaded the Glamorgan committee to play at The Gnoll, and in June 1908 Neath staged its first Minor County fixture, with Glamorgan defeating Carmarthenshire by an innings and one run.

Neath continued to stage an annual Minor County fixture until after the First World War. By this time, the Gnoll Estate was owned by the Neath Corporation, and in 1923 they resisted the temptation to sell the land for building, deciding instead that the ruins of the Gnoll House should be the town's war memorial, and that the rugby and cricket ground should be preserved for sporting activities.

Neath Corporation were responsible for The Gnoll staging first-class cricket. In the 1930s they offered various financial incentives to Glamorgan if the county agreed to play a Championship fixture at the ground. With the club's finances in turmoil, their officials were ready to explore any new venture, and they allocated the 1934 fixture with Essex to The Gnoll. It proved to be a well-attended game, and Neath was duly added to the club's fixture list. The annual fixtures proved very popular, with 12,000 people watching the

Play in progress at The Gnoll in 1906 as the Gentlemen of Glamorgan entertain the Gentlemen of Essex.

match with Warwickshire in 1948.

In the early 1950s, Glamorgan decided to build an indoor school at Neath, hoping that the purpose-built complex would act as the club's winter coaching base in the west. On 28 October 1954, the indoor school was opened by Bob Wyatt, and over the following years, a host of young Glamorgan cricketers were groomed in the nets over the winter months and the fine facilities were used by the county club in their pre-season activities.

Despite the improved facilities, there were a few difficulties, especially when it rained. The area around The Gnoll has a high water-table, and some people believe the area was once the former course of the River Neath. There are several small springs on the hillside below the remains of Mackworth's old mansion, and the result was that the ground took a long time to dry out after rain; consequently, in the late 1960s the ground was used for one-day matches rather than three-day Championship games. Indeed, in 1969 Neath hosted Glamorgan's first-ever home game in the Sunday League. Even these limited overs matches were often rain affected, and after the Benson & Hedges Cup fixture with Gloucestershire had taken three days to complete in 1974, The Gnoll was dropped from the county's First XI fixture list.

During the early 1980s, various industrial regeneration schemes were started, and the Neath Development Partnership began to promote tourism and recreation in the area. They viewed county cricket as the perfect vehicle for promoting their activities and the area as well, so in 1984 Neath Borough Council offered Glamorgan a substantial sponsorship package if the Australian match in 1985 was staged at The Gnoll. The offer of around £320,000 resulted in the tourist match being staged at The Gnoll, and the game saw Javed Miandad and Younis Ahmed add 306* for the third wicket, with Javed hitting a brilliant double-century.

The success of the game and the off-field arrangements led to Glamorgan playing further first-class and limited overs cricket at the ground, in addition to the 1989 and 1993 matches with the Australians, plus the 1995 fixture with the Australian 'A' side. Amongst the one-day games held at Neath was the 1990 Sunday League fixture with Somerset, whose all-rounder Graham Rose hit a rapid 148 with seven mighty sixes. His 46-ball century, plus an unbeaten 136 from Jimmy Cook, saw Somerset to 360-3 – the highest ever total in the competition against Glamorgan.

A Neath CC team group in 1912.

GROUND STATISTICS FOR NEATH

First first-class match   *v.* Essex, 14, 15 and 16 July 1934

Most recent first-class match   *v.* Australia A, 8, 9 and 10 July 1995

First limited overs match   *v.* Worcestershire, 12 June, 1963

Most recent limited overs match   *v.* Leicestershire, 28 August, 1994

Playing Record

	P	W	L	D	Ab/NR
County Championship	39	12	11	16	-
First-class friendlies	3	-	-	3	-
Gillette Cup	2	1	1		-
Benson and Hedges	1	-	1		-
Sunday League	9	4	5		-

Two of Neath's most famous cricketers – Tom Whittington (left) who became Glamorgan's secretary and guided the county into the County Championship in 1921, and Cyril Walters (right) who went on to play for Worcestershire and England.

FIRST-CLASS BATTING RECORDS AT NEATH

Highest Team Total

By Glamorgan	409-3 dec	v. Australians, 1985
Against Glamorgan	347-4 dec	by Warwickshire, 1959

Lowest Team Total

By Glamorgan	43	v. Essex, 1935
Against Glamorgan	57	by Surrey, 1937

Highest Individual Score

By Glamorgan	200*	Javed Miandad	v. Australians, 1985
Against Glamorgan	219*	G.A. Hick	for Worcestershire, 1986

Highest Partnership

By Glamorgan	306*	Javed Miandad and Younis Ahmed for the 4th wkt v. Australians, 1985
Against Glamorgan	287*	G.A. Hick and T.S. Curtis for the 2nd wkt for Worcestershire, 1986

Younis Ahmed.   Javed Miandad.

LIMITED OVERS BATTING RECORDS AT NEATH

Highest Team Total

| By Glamorgan | 210-5 | v. Leicestershire, 1994 |
| Against Glamorgan | 360-3 | by Somerset, 1990 |

Lowest Team Total

| By Glamorgan | 90 | v. Yorkshire, 1969 |
| Against Glamorgan | 91-6 | by Yorkshire, 1969 |

Highest Individual Score

| By Glamorgan | 78 | E.J. Lewis | v. Worcestershire, 1963 |
| Against Glamorgan | 148 | G.D. Rose | for Somerset, 1990 |

Highest Partnership

| By Glamorgan | 76 | R.C. Ontong and G.C. Holmes for the 4th wkt v. Essex, 1987 |
| Against Glamorgan | 223 | S.J. Cook and G.D. Rose for the 3rd wkt for Somerset, 1990 |

Tony Lewis – another of the famous cricketers to have been brought up in Neath. After leaving the town's famous grammar school, Tony played for Glamorgan from 1955 until 1974, and was their inspirational captain when they won the Championship in 1969. Tony also led England in their Tests against India and Pakistan in 1972/73.

BOWLING RECORDS AT NEATH

Best bowling in an innings in first-class cricket

| For Glamorgan | 8-48 | B.L. Muncer | v. Somerset, 1949 |
| Against Glamorgan | 9-39 | D.J. Halfyard | for Kent, 1957 |

Best bowling in a match in first-class cricket

| For Glamorgan | 12-94 | B.L. Muncer | v. Somerset, 1949 |
| Against Glamorgan | 13-51 | A.E. Moss | for Middlesex, 1960 |

Best bowling in a limited overs match

| For Glamorgan | 5-36 | S.R. Barwick | v. Leicestershire, 1994 |
| Against | 5-43 | J.A. Flavell | for Worcestershire, 1963 |

Mark Frost, in action during Glamorgan's match against Leicestershire at Neath in 1991. The rugby ground can be seen in the background.

8

RODNEY PARADE, NEWPORT

Monmouthshire was one of the early centres of cricket in Wales. The first record of cricket in Newport dates from 1820, and within four years, a Monmouthshire side was in existence. The county club was actually largely a gentleman's club, based at The Beaufort Arms in Raglan. However, its success was an indication that many good players lived and worked in the vicinity of Newport,

In 1834 a formal club was established in Newport, which played on land in a field off Marshes Road (on the west bank of the River Usk to the north of the town centre, near what subsequently became known as Shaftesbury Park). As trade from the town's port increased, so did the number of members, as well as the number of cricket teams in the Newport area. However, the Newport club was the premier side, and it secured fixtures with Cardiff and Swansea, besides leading English clubs such as Gloucester, Ross, Hereford and Clifton.

By the early 1850s, one of their leading lights was George Homfray, a member of the family of industrialists who owned ironworks in Merthyr, Ebbw Vale and Tredegar. Homfray was instrumental in organising a grand match in Newport during 1858 between a Monmouthshire side and the All England XI. The game attracted a large crowd, with the local newspaper reporting that the road leading to the ground, off Marshes Road, 'was densely crowded, with fruit and ginger beer stalls pitched along the sidewalks. The taverns and beer houses all did a thriving business along the road during the match.'

In 1875, the Newport Athletic Club was created with the amalgamation of the town's cricket, tennis, rugby and athletics organisations. Two years later, they secured the lease of seven acres of land, owned by Lord Tredegar at Rodney Parade, on the east bank of the Usk, to the south of Newport Bridge. Over the next few years, various small-scale improvements took place as Lord Tredegar encouraged the creation of a proper facility for the town's young sportsmen.

In the early 1880s, the Rodney Parade sports ground boasted one of the best wickets in the area and hosted some of the home games organised by the South Wales CC. In September 1881, it also staged the game between a Newport and District XXII and an All England XI captained by Dr W.G. Grace, during which the doctor returned the fine match bowling figures of 70.1-27-74-22.

All of the club's athletic pursuits had initially taken place on the one sports field, but in the mid-1890s, Lord Tredegar leased a further five acres of land to the Athletic Club, allowing a self-contained cricket ground to be laid out with a purpose-built pavilion, terrace seating, and a scoreboard. The work was completed by 1901, and on 1 June Lord Tredegar formally opened the new Rodney Parade cricket ground, and a special game was staged against Cardiff CC.

In 1892, Fred Phillips, a member of the well-known Newport brewing family, created the Monmouthshire County Cricket Association. Phillips believed that there were enough good players in the area to form a proper, and representative, county side which could follow Glamorgan into the Minor County Championship.

Phillips was fortunate enough to call upon the services of a number of professionals attached to the Newport club. The athletic club's finances allowed up to three cricket professionals to be hired each year, plus eight groundstaff, largely as a result of the success of the rugby team. In 1893, over £2,000 was taken in gate receipts at the rugby matches, allowing the athletic club to hire good former county professionals including Dick Steeples, formerly of Derbyshire and Edwin Diver, the former Surrey and Warwickshire wicketkeeper.

However, Newport's most successful professional was Arthur Silverlock, a fine all-rounder

Rodney Parade – as seen in 1964, with in the background, the impressive pavilion, built in 1901.

who took 8-78 for Monmouthshire as Glamorgan were defeated by six wickets in 1894. The following year, Silverlock scored 120 and took 16 wickets in Monmouthshire's victory over Herefordshire. With other good victories in the subsequent years, Phillips was able to contact the MCC and apply for Monmouthshire to join the Minor County Championship.

In 1901 Monmouthshire were admitted to the Minor County competition, and the Rodney Parade ground became their home base. However, they suffered a rather unfortunate start to their new career with a pair of innings defeats against rivals Glamorgan. In the match at the Arms Park, Herbie Morgan lashed the Monmouthshire attack for 254 as Glamorgan raced to 538, but there were mitigating circumstances as Monmouthshire started the game without four team members who had been delayed by a train accident in the Newport tunnel.

Things soon improved, and in 1905 Monmouthshire finished second in the table, after some fine batting displays from Edward Stone Phillips, another member of the brewing family, who had won a blue at Cambridge the previous year. Despite becoming a director of the brewery, Phillips found plenty of time to play for both Newport and Monmouthshire, hitting 133* against Glamorgan in 1905, and 150 against the same opponents in the following year.

It was largely through the efforts of Phillips, Steeples and Silverlock, that Monmouthshire enjoyed success as a Minor County either side of the First World War.

In 1922, the freehold of the entire Rodney Parade complex was purchased by the athletic club, and a number of further improvements were made to both the cricket ground and the adjoining rugby pitch, whilst memorial gates were erected in memory of the athletic club's members who had died in the First World War. The facilities at Rodney Parade were on a par with those at the Arms Park, and there were several people associated with both Newport Athletic Club and the Monmouthshire club who hoped that the county side might one day follow Glamorgan into the County Championship.

But on the field, things were not going as smoothly, and just as the Newport ground was becoming one of the best equipped in the area, Monmouthshire CCC languished at the bottom of the Minor County table. Tenth place in 1927 was their highest position, and the lack of success was converted into major financial worries. Several of the town's businesses also fell on hard times as trade from

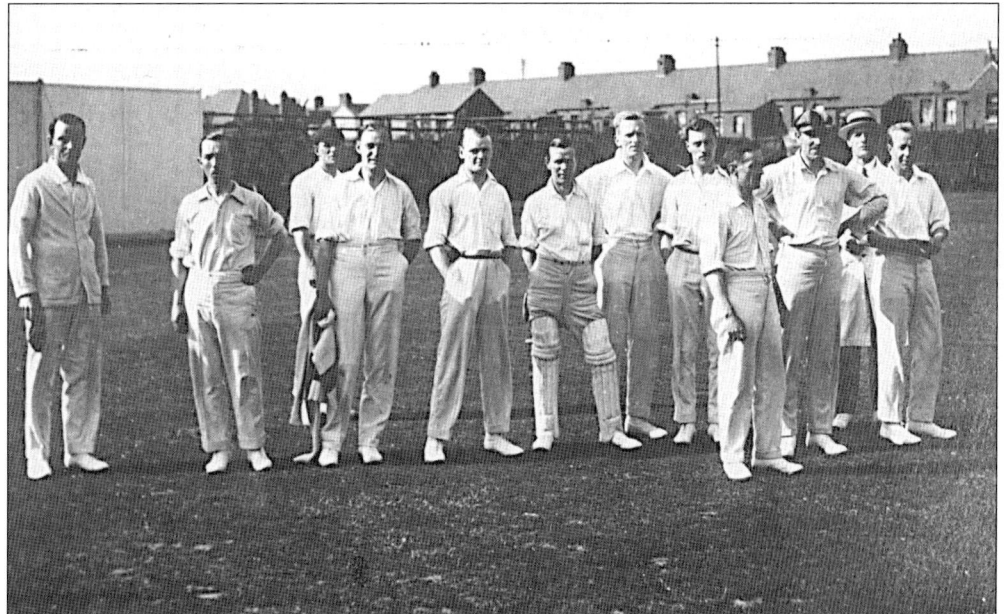

A Monmouthshire CCC team group in 1930.

Newport Docks, like the other ports on Severnside, started to decline.

With an ever-growing debt, Monmouthshire were unable to afford decent professionals, and their playing record deteriorated even further. Noises were made to the Glamorgan committee about an affiliation, but they too were struggling for cash and a merger was out of the question. By the end of the 1933 season, even more drastic cost-cutting measures had been introduced as Monmouthshire could barely afford the cost of travel and hotel fees for away games.

Further approaches were made by T.B. Wiilliams, the influential captain of Newport, to Maurice Turnbull, Glamorgan's highly respected captain and secretary, plus Johnnie Clay, their stalwart spinner and honorary treasurer. It did not take Williams long to convince both of the Glamorgan men that a merger between the two counties would be of great benefit to Glamorgan. Firstly, it would help them further raise their standing as the county side representing South Wales, and they could take county cricket to potentially quite lucrative venues in Newport and the surrounding area. In addition, the merger would allow Glamorgan to field a Second XI in the Minor County competition and groom young players, thereby helping the club in the long run from relying on hiring rejects and has-beens from other counties. Turnbull and Clay were able to give serious consideration to the approach as Glamorgan's finances were now in a slightly better position. A draft proposal was subsequently agreed upon in July 1934 and the two counties merged. In return for clearing Monmouthshire's debts, Glamorgan were allowed to select any of the Monmouthshire players, and stage at least two Championship fixtures each year in Monmouthshire.

In July 1935, Glamorgan played their first game at their 'new' ground at Rodney Parade. Leicestershire were Glamorgan's first opponents at the Newport ground, and before play commenced on 6 July, both teams were presented to the town's Lord Mayor. On the Saturday evening, a lavish civic reception was held in the town hall, and the following day, players from both teams were taken by omnibus on a special tour of the picturesque Wye Valley. After the previous night's celebrations, the tour probably helped to clear a few hangovers.

Perhaps the most famous County Championship game ever staged at Rodney Parade was the 1939 encounter between Glamorgan and Gloucestershire. The home team batted first and made a modest 196, before Wally Hammond led a single-handed assault on the Glamorgan bowlers, making a majestic 302 – at the time, a record score against the Welsh side.

Time and again, Hammond unfurled his classical cover drives, sending the ball speeding to the boundary ropes almost before the Glamorgan could blink an eye. In all, the Gloucestershire maestro hit 35 fours, plus 2 enormous sixes, one of which sailed through a window high up on the

A scorecard for one of Monmouthshire's Minor County fixtures.

68

power station alongside the ground. Local legend has it that in memory of what many regarded as the finest innings they had ever seen, the window was never repaired, with the small round hole through which the ball passed remaining there for twenty-five years until the building was demolished in the mid 1960s. After their mauling by Hammond, Glamorgan needed the small matter of 309 runs in order to avoid an innings defeat when they batted again on the second afternoon. The instructions from captain Maurice Turnbull were to concentrate on batting throughout the rest of the match and, in typically phlegmatic style, Emrys Davies and Arnold Dyson shared an opening stand of 255, which proved that despite their modest first innings performance, there really were no gremlins in the Newport wicket. Despite the loss of Dyson, Davies remained unflappable, and he duly reached 150 on the final afternoon as Glamorgan moved closer to their target. With the Gloucestershire bowlers starting to tire and the wicket continuing to play in a true way, MauriceTurnbull suggested to Davies that he should set his sights on passing Dick Duckfield's county record of 280 and then possibly become the first Glamorgan batsman to score 300. There was also another incentive for the batsmen that summer, with a special prize on offer for the highest score of the season. Hammond's triple hundred had passed the previous best, so with the encouragement of his colleagues ringing in his ears, Davies set out to beat Hammond's 302. With Maurice Turnbull deftly rotating the strike, Davies reached his double-hundred, and thanks to support from Dai Davies, Emrys had reached 250 as the game entered its final stages. By this time, the Glamorgan supporters were hoping that they might see Davies score the first ever triple-hundred for the club, and register the season's highest season. But Hammond also had his eye on the special prize and the kudos it carried. With time starting to slip away from Emrys, Hammond slowed down the Glamorgan batsman's progress by employing far more defensive fields. By the time Emrys had set a new club record on 281, most of the Gloucestershire fielders were out in the deep to prevent any more

balls going for a boundary. A physically exhausted Davies was happy to remain unbeaten on 287, and he received a standing ovation as he wearily made his way off the ground after the umpires called time. However, many of the home supporters were non-plussed at the actions of Hammond, and they vented their feelings by shouting a few ribald comments in his direction as he came off the pitch. At the time, Hammond was the England captain and many of the supporters felt it was rather unbecoming of someone of that standing employing negative tactics to deny one of the local heroes from reaching a landmark in a game that was petering out into a draw.

Left: Wally Hammond. Right:
Emrys Davies.

GROUND STATISTICS FOR NEWPORT

First first-class match   *v.* Leicestershire, 6, 8, 9 July 1935

Final first-class match   *v.* Warwickshire, 5, 6, 7 May 1965

First limited overs match   *v.* Worcestershire, 25 April 1964

Final limited overs match   *v.* Yorkshire, 24 June 1990

Playing Record

	P	W	L	D	Ab/NR
County Championship	25	7	9	9	-
First-class friendlies	2	2	-	-	-
Gillette/NatWest/C&G	1	1	-		-
Sunday League	3	1	1		1

A deserted Rodney Parade in the mid-1980s.

FIRST-CLASS BATTING RECORDS AT NEWPORT

Highest Team Total

| By Glamorgan | 577-4 | v. Gloucestershire, 1939 |
| Against Glamorgan | 505-5 dec | by Gloucestershire, 1939 |

Lowest Team Total

| By Glamorgan | 69 | v. Yorkshire, 1949 |
| Against Glamorgan | 69 | by Sir Julian Cahn's XI, 1938 |

Highest Individual Score

| By Glamorgan | 287* | D.E. Davies | v. Gloucestershire, 1939 |
| Against Glamorgan | 302 | W.R. Hammond | for Gloucestershire, 1939 |

Highest Partnership

| By Glamorgan | 255 | D. E. Davies and A. H. Dyson for the 1st wkt v. Gloucestershire, 1939 |
| Against Glamorgan | 214 | W.R. Hammond and J.F. Crapp for the 5th wkt for Gloucestershire, 1939 |

The Nottinghamshire team taking the field for their Championship match with Glamorgan at Rodney Parade in 1961.

BOWLING RECORDS AT RODNEY PARADE, NEWPORT

Best bowling in an innings in first-class cricket

| For Glamorgan | 7-74 | J.E. McConnon | v. Essex, 1960 |
| Against Glamorgan | 9-77 | D. Shackleton | for Hampshire, 1953 |

Best bowling in a match in first-class cricket

| For Glamorgan | 13-188 | J.C. Clay | v. Somerset, 1937 |
| Against Glamorgan | 13-99 | T.W. Goddard | for Gloucestershire, 1937 |

Best bowling in a limited overs match

| For Glamorgan | 3-12 | D.J. Shepherd | v. Worcestershire, 1964 |
| Against | 4-25 | J.A. Flavell | for Worcestershire, 1964 |

Jim McConnon.

Tom Goddard.

LIMITED OVERS BATTING RECORDS AT RODNEY PARADE, NEWPORT

Highest Team Total

| By Glamorgan | 199-8 | *v.* Derbyshire, 1988 |
| Against Glamorgan | 174 | by Derbyshire, 1988 |

Lowest Team Total

| By Glamorgan | 120-9 | *v.* Worcestershire, 1964 |
| Against Glamorgan | 119 | by Worcestershire, 1964 |

Highest Individual Score

| By Glamorgan | 60 | J.A. Hopkins | *v.* Derbyshire, 1988 |
| Against Glamorgan | 90* | K.J. Barnett | for Derbyshire, 1988 |

Highest Partnership

| By Glamorgan | 86 | A.R. Butcher and H. Morris for the 1st wkt *v.* Gloucestershire, 1989 |
| Against Glamorgan | 56 | A.J. Wright and C.W.J. Athey for the 1st wkt for Gloucestershire, 1989 |

John Hopkins.

When county cricket resumed after the Second World War, Rodney Parade remained on Glamorgan's fixture list, but despite the prospect of watching the county's stars in action again, the matches at Newport attracted quite disappointing crowds. Their game against Somerset in 1948, their Championship-winning year, brought in just £105, compared with £550 on the first day of the Essex match at the Arms Park.

Consequently, Newport was allocated just one fixture, with the other 'Monmouthshire' match being given to Ebbw Vale. Even so, the games at Newport in the 1950s were not as well supported as before the war, and the Newport wickets started to give more assistance to the county bowlers. No longer were they the veritable featherbeds they had been in the pre-war days, as Derek Shackleton took 9-77 for Hampshire in 1953.

The drop in county attendances was a national trend, as people found other outlets for their leisure time. But as far as Glamorgan were concerned, their ever-worsening financial situation meant that they had to keep a close eye on the cost of playing at Newport, especially if other more lucrative venues became available. In an attempt to boost interest in county games at Newport, Glamorgan experimented by staging their Gillette Cup match against Worcestershire in April 1964 at the Rodney Parade ground.

It proved to be quite a nail-biting contest with Glamorgan eventually winning by one wicket, and all in front of the BBC television cameras, but only after Don Shepherd had struck a huge six off the fourth ball of the 65th and final over. The off-spinner had taken three wickets as Worcestershire were dismissed for 119, and he deservedly won the man of the match award for his efforts with bat and ball.

However, the contest was played on a damp pitch and a mix of drizzle and April showers made it far from ideal cricket-watching weather. Not surprisingly, the game did not produce the sort of crowd the Glamorgan officials had hoped for, and the following year, the Championship match with Warwickshire also failed to attract a decent crowd. With the club deciding to take county games to the North Wales coast, a few savings had to made elsewhere, and Rodney Parade lost its first-class status.

For the next twenty years, the Newport ground only staged second-team games, but county matches returned in 1988 as the county celebrated their Centenary year. A generous sponsorship package from local businesses saw Glamorgan return to Newport for their Sunday League games against Derbyshire in 1988, and also Gloucestershire in 1989, and Yorkshire in 1990. The latter game was abandoned without a ball being bowled and it proved to be a rather damp way for the county to say farewell to their Newport home following the confirmation that the cricket ground and pavilion had been sold for redevelopment.

Building work began at the end of the 1990 season, as the cricket section of the Newport Athletic Club moved to a new ground in Spytty Park to the north of the town centre. In 1997, Glamorgan paid their first visit to the new ground for their Bain Hogg Second XI match against Gloucestershire Second XI. The Wales Minor Counties side have also played at the Spytty Park ground, against Shropshire and Wiltshire in 1998, as well as Herefordshire in 1999.

9

EUGENE CROSS PARK, EBBW VALE

Eugene Cross Park, Ebbw Vale is another of Glamorgan's venues which doubles up as both a rugby and cricket ground. In contrast to the St Helen's ground in Swansea, there is little overlap in terms of playing area. The cricket square lies in the northern half of the park, and the rugby pitch occupies the southern section of the ground, both nestling in the hollow-like valley of the Ebbw River between Beaufort Road and New Church Road.

Despite their modern day co-existence, cricket predates rugby in this steel-making town in the Gwent Valleys. The first record of a cricket match taking place in Ebbw Vale dates from 1852, when a fixture was held with Blaenau. This was some seventy years after Edward Kendall had established a furnace for iron and steel making, using the local raw materials and charcoal by burning felled trees from the densely wooded slopes of the Ebbw Valley.

The further expansion of steel-making in the area, plus the influx of migrants from surrounding counties of England and Wales, gave cricket a further boost during the middle of the nineteenth century. Despite the restrictions imposed by the regular shifts, there were several teams in the town by the 1870s. One of these was a team of schoolmasters, and the introduction of organised games into the school curriculum meant that more of the local youngsters learnt the rudiments of the game. Support also came from the various religious leaders who, as believers in Muscular Christianity, considered that the playing of games helped to give order and moral structure to life within the tightly knit and drink-ridden industrial communities.

By the end of the nineteenth century, there was enough support for cricket within the town of Ebbw Vale for a formal club to be created. They secured the use of a field alongside the Ebbw

River, close to the Bridgend Hotel, and by the First World War, the 'Bridgend Field' had become the town's major area for recreation, being used for association football and rugby, in addition to cricket.

The Ebbw Vale Steel, Iron and Coal Company realised that it was important for their employees to have the chance to partake in healthy recreation, so in November 1919 they formed the Ebbw Vale Welfare Association and bought the Bridgend Field from Phillips Brewery. The six acres of land became known as the Welfare Association Ground, and in 1973 its name was changed to its present title in honour of Sir Eugene Cross, the influential and longstanding chairman of the Welfare Trustees.

In 1920, a cricket pavilion was erected to the north of the cricket field, whilst a rugby grandstand was built in the southern part of the ground, alongside the Bridgend Hotel. In June of that year, Glamorgan visited the Ebbw Vale ground for a two-day friendly with Monmouthshire, and in August 1921, Monmouthshire staged their first Minor County Championship match at Ebbw Vale with Dorset providing the opposition.

The Ebbw Vale ground continued to stage some of Monmouthshire's Minor County matches in the 1920s and 1930s, and their merger with Glamorgan in 1934 opened up the possibility of the Welfare Ground staging County Championship matches. However, the trade depression of the 1930s and the slump in the steel trade resulted in a rise in unemployment in the Ebbw Valley, so the Glamorgan officials decided to continue staging Minor County fixtures at the Welfare Association ground. These began in August 1935 with Glamorgan's Second XI fixture with Dorset, followed by the matches with Cheshire in 1936 and Middlesex Second XI in 1937. The decision by Richard Thomas and Baldwins to rebuild their furnaces and modernise their steel plant in Ebbw Vale, plus the increase in orders after the Second World War, gave the town a lift after the war, so when Glamorgan regrouped in 1946, and thought about tapping support at new venues, the county's officials decided to experiment by adding the Welfare Ground to their fixture list.

The inaugural first-class match took place at the ground in June 1946 against Worcestershire, and a first-day crowd of 5,000 vindicated the committee's decision to take county cricket into

A view of Ebbw Vale in the early 1900s.

the Ebbw Valley. Johnnie Clay, the county's veteran captain, was delighted by the way everything had gone so smoothly, so after the game, he wrote to the Welfare Association saying 'the match was a sensational success, as apart from the fine crowd, the arrangements made to deal with it were quite magnificent. It would appear now that Ebbw Vale as a centre of first-class cricket is very much on the map.'

Nor were these hollow words of praise, as later in the season, there were difficulties preparing a wicket at Stradey Park, and the Nottinghamshire game was switched from Llanelli to the Welfare Ground. In the years up until 1968, the Ebbw Vale ground staged an annual Championship fixture, but there were concerns over the state of the wicket, which too often assisted the spin bowlers. After the match with Nottinghamshire in August 1967, the wicket was reported by the umpires as being unfit for first-class cricket, and the ground was subsequently dropped from the county's Championship calendar.

The introduction of the John Player League from 1969 saw the ground return to the county circuit by staging an annual Sunday game. Its compact size made the Welfare Ground an ideal venue for one-day games and since 1969, the crowds, often in excess of 5,000, have been treated to some swashbuckling innings, with balls regularly being deposited high onto the grassed embankment on the eastern side of the ground or over the trees lining the western boundary alongside the River Ebbw. Even so, there were some fine bowling performances in the limited-overs contests, with Graham Kingston taking 6-36 against Derbyshire in the inaugural Sunday fixture in 1969.

In 1981, a new organisation called the Ebbw Vale Recreation Grounds Trust and Institute was created to take over the place of the Welfare Association, and they took over the ownership of the ground. Championship cricket made a brief return to the ground in 1983 after some local sponsorship, but in 1984 there was a switch back to Sunday League games, with Geoff Holmes taking 5 wickets for just 2 runs, including a hat-trick, in the match against Nottinghamshire. In 1990, Ebbw Vale hosted the county's three-day friendly with the Sri Lankans, before reverting to staging an annual Sunday League match. Since 1996, the ground has been used solely for second-team fixtures.

The Welfare Ground.

With an altitude of around 878 feet above sea level, the Ebbw Vale ground is the highest of all of Glamorgan's ground. Its altitude and location, close to several upland sheep farms, has led to some unusual incidents. For example in August 1948 the first day of the Championship match against Gloucestershire was halted as a mist rolled down the hillsides and enshrouded the ground. It hung around for most of the afternoon, before lifting to reveal a flock of sheep all over the outfield.

Peter Walker, the Glamorgan and England all-rounder, also recalls the time when he was batting at the Welfare Ground, and marking his guard at the crease. 'After speaking to the umpire, I used the toe of my bat to mark my guard, and then used the bat to tap down a few areas on the wicket. You can imagine my surprise when a loud banging sound echoed back from underground, no doubt from a miner working in one of the mines!'

The ground has also seen some fine performances by Glamorgan players, including in 1949 a scintillating hundred in just 79 minutes by Phil Clift which saw the Welsh county to a well deserved nine-wicket victory. In 1964, Don Shepherd returned the remarkable figures of 10-8-2-5 against Leicestershire, whilst four years later Ossie Wheatley took 9-60 in the Championship game against Sussex.

A number of illustrious cricketers have been hired over the years as professionals by the Ebbw Vale club. Percy Holmes, Harold Gimblett, and Bill Andrews are three of the famous English cricketers to be attached to the club, for whom a close association with the steelworks meant that plenty of money was available to hire decent professionals.

Several of the club's players including Len Pitchford, Wilf Hughes, Jack Cope and G. B. Shaw have also gone on to play for Glamorgan. Pitchford hit a double-century for Glamorgan against Berkshire in 1935, whilst Hughes had a most dramatic entry into first-class cricket, sharing a match-saving partnership of 131 with Cyril Smart for the tenth wicket against the 1935 South Africans, and belying his position at number eleven in the order by smashing an unbeaten 70, including four huge sixes.

George Shaw was an off-spinner, with a high slow loop, who joined the county's playing staff in the late 1940s. He played for the county until 1955, when he returned to play for Ebbw Vale in 1964. By this time, the Indoor School, on the eastern side of the ground had been opened, and which was opened during the 1950s alongside the pavilion, and this has been a popular base for the county's winter coaching programme in the Gwent Valleys.

Gloucestershire's Tom Pugh (left) and Barrie Meyer (right) walk to the wicket to resume their partnership during the Championship match with Glamorgan at Ebbw Vale in 1960.

GROUND STATISTICS FOR EBBW VALE

First first-class match   *v.* Worcestershire, June 22, 24, 25, 1946

Most recent first-class match   *v.* Sri Lankans, August 22, 23, 24, 1990

First limited overs match   *v.* Derbyshire, August 10, 1969

Most recent limited overs match   *v.* Worcestershire, May 26, 1996

Playing Record

	P	W	L	D	Ab/NR
County Championship	24	9	3	12	-
First-class friendlies	1	-	-	1	-
Sunday League	26	11	12		3

The Welfare Ground in Ebbw Vale, with the rugby ground in the foreground and the cricket pitch in the distance.

FIRST-CLASS BATTING RECORDS AT EBBW VALE

Highest Team Total

By Glamorgan   355-9 dec   v. Sri Lankans, 1990
Against Glamorgan   354-9 dec   by Essex, 1954

Lowest Team Total

By Glamorgan   64   v. Essex, 1962
Against Glamorgan   33   by Leicestershire, 1965

Highest Individual Score

By Glamorgan   126   H. Morris   v. Sri Lankans, 1990
Against Glamorgan   132   H. Horton   for Hampshire, 1959

Highest Partnership

By Glamorgan   191   H. Morris and G.C. Holmes for the 4th wkt v. Sri Lankans, 1990
Against Glamorgan   144   D.M. Young and C.A. Milton for the 1st wkt for
                          Gloucestershire, 1952

Hugh Morris.

Geoff Holmes.

BOWLING RECORDS AT EBBW VALE

Best bowling in an innings in first-class cricket

For Glamorgan	9-60	O.S. Wheatley	v. Sussex, 1968
Against Glamorgan	6-29	K.C. Preston	for Essex, 1962

Best bowling in a match in first-class cricket

For Glamorgan	11-115	O.S. Wheatley	v. Sussex, 1968
Against Glamorgan	10-97	K. C. Preston	for Essex, 1962

Best bowling in a limited overs match

For Glamorgan	6-36	G.C. Kingston	v. Derbyshire, 1969
Against Glamorgan	5-13	J.K. Lever	for Essex, 1975

A view of the Sunday League match between Glamorgan and Sussex at Ebbw Vale in 1981.

LIMITED OVERS BATTING RECORDS AT EBBW VALE

Highest Team Total

By Glamorgan	277-6	*v.* Derbyshire, 1984
Against Glamorgan	241-7	by Sussex, 1981

Lowest Team Total

By Glamorgan	92	*v.* Derbyshire, 1974
Against Glamorgan	96	by Derbyshire, 1969

Highest Individual Score

By Glamorgan	103*	Younis Ahmed	*v.* Derbyshire, 1984
Against Glamorgan	80	N.E. Briers	for Leicestershire, 1980
		A.R. Butcher	for Surrey, 1977

Highest Partnership

By Glamorgan	147	Younis Ahmed and Javed Miandad for the 3rd wkt *v.* Derbys, 1984
Against Glamorgan	90	R.D.V. Knight and D.M. Smith for the 4th wkt for Surrey, 1979

Alan Butcher, seen here in his days with Surrey. He subsequently joined Glamorgan in 1987 and led them with distinction between 1989 and 1992.

10
STEEL COMPANY OF WALES, MARGAM

The Steel Company of Wales ground at Margam played host to three championship matches and two other first-class friendlies between 1953 and 1963. The ground is part of the company's purpose-built recreational complex, half a mile to the south of the village of Margam, and close to the town of Port Talbot.

The sporting complex itself lies in between the M4 motorway to the north and the Margam Abbey works to the south, which were formerly owned by British Steel, now Corus, and run in tandem with the giant Llanwern Works to the east of Newport.

The ground also lies near Margam Park, the home of the Fox-Talbot family, who organised games of country house cricket in the second half of the nineteenth century. Annual matches were staged against other gentlemen's XIs, including the Jersey Estate XI, sides raised by other members of the local gentry, such as J.T.D. Llewelyn of Penllegaer and the Bransby Williams family of Killay House.

In 1923, the Margam Abbey Works were opened, and shortly afterwards, a cricket club was formed. Originally called Port Talbot Steelworks CC, they played in a field close to the Twelve Knights pub in Margam village, before moving to a purpose-built ground in 1946. This followed the acquisition by the Steel Company of Wales of 40 acres of farmland for a recreational complex, and in 1947 the cricket club's name was changed to S.C.O.W. Margam, as the company spent money on providing decent sports and social facilities for their employees.

In addition to laying a new square, facilities were provided for rugby, soccer, hockey, golf, bowls and tennis, whilst a sports and social club was built, comprising ten changing rooms on the ground floor, plus a lounge, bar and concert hall upstairs. Originally, the cricket square was located in front of the sports and social club, and this was where the county games were played. However, the square was subsequently moved further away, to allow the rugby pitch to occupy the land in front of the clubhouse, and a small cricket pavilion was built adjacent to the re-sited wicket.

The decision by Glamorgan to take first-class cricket to the Margam ground during the 1950s followed the offer of financial support from the Steel Company of Wales. At the time, the county club were eager to boost their funds, and also help finance decent coaching and practice facilities at a number of clubs throughout South Wales. In 1951, the Glamorgan Club and Ground XI played for the first time at the ground, and after being impressed with the purpose-built facilities, the county's officials accepted the offer of support from S.C.O.W. and allocated their friendly with the Gentlemen of Ireland in 1953 to the Margam ground.

The match against the Gentlemen of Ireland took place over the Whitsun Bank Holiday and, in anticipation of a sizeable crowd, 5,000 seats were installed, marquees were erected and a brand new scoreboard was built by the apprentices from the Steel Company of Wales works. However, there was nothing anyone could do about the weather and rain washed out the first day's play in addition to interrupting proceedings on the other two days as well. Consequently, play took place on a damp wicket, and batting not surprisingly was something of a lottery, with *Wisden*'s correspondent describing the conditions as 'a nightmare for batsmen.' Glamorgan made 81 and 81-6, whilst the Irish amateurs replied with 67 and 81-9, so the match ended in a draw.

The Glamorgan officials were naturally concerned about the quality of the Margam

The Gentlemen of Ireland pictured with the Glamorgan side before their fixture at Margam in 1953.

wicket, so it was not until 1960, and only after remedial work had been undertaken to the square, that county cricket returned to the steelworks ground. In that year, it staged the Championship match with Sussex, followed by matches with Leicestershire in 1961, Gloucestershire in 1962 and Cambridge University in 1963.

The wicket played a lot better in these games, but even so, the attendances were fairly modest, and there were problems as well with smoke billowing over the ground from the steel complex. Indeed, in the match with Cambridge University in 1963, the students appealed against the conditions as a series of smoke plumes descended on the ground as they were trying to save the game.

The smoke eventually cleared, but a more pressing concern was the low attendances at these games. Despite the support from the Steel Company of Wales, it was relatively expensive for the county to stage fixtures at the ground, and it was located away from any built-up area. Moreover, the whole area was open to the elements, and players and spectators often complained about the squally winds that blew across the unprotected area.

After the university game in 1964, Jack Morgan wrote 'there was something unreal about the cricket at Margam. Perhaps the strangest thing of all was that on the match was played on a ground completely deserted. It was certainly an eerie atmosphere and Glamorgan must seriously consider whether it is worthwhile giving Margam another fixture. The ground is not only exposed to the weather, but is inconveniently situated and this must interfere with the attendance.' The gate receipts bore out his point – £70 was taken on the first day, £35 on the second and nothing at all on the final day. It came as no great surprise that Margam was deleted from the first-class calendar in 1964.

The ground has continued to stage Second XI games, and the club have played with success in the South Wales Cricket Association. Amongst the Glamorgan professionals to have been attached to the club are Euros Lewis, Alan Rees and Don Ward. Alan Durban also played for the side in 1959 and 1960 whilst on the county's staff, before concentrating on a career as a footballer and, in more recent times, a football manager.

GROUND STATISTICS FOR MARGAM

First first-class match   *v*. Gentlemen of Ireland, 1953

Final first-class match   *v*. Cambridge University, 1963

Playing Record

	P	W	L	D
County Championship	3	1	1	1
First-class friendlies	2	-	-	2

Highest Team Total
By Glamorgan	298	*v*. Cambridge University, 1963
Against Glamorgan	161	by Sussex, 1960

Lowest Team Total
By Glamorgan	49	*v*. Gloucestershire, 1962
Against Glamorgan	67	by Gentlemen of Ireland, 1953

Highest Individual Innings
By Glamorgan	90	B. Hedges	*v*. Cambridge University, 1963
Against Glamorgan	54	E.J. Craig	for Cambridge University, 1963

Best bowling in an innings
By Glamorgan	7-32	J.B. Evans	*v*. Leicestershire, 1961
Against Glamorgan	5-10	J.B. Mortimore	for Gloucestershire, 1962

Best bowling in a match
By Glamorgan	11-51	D.J. Shepherd	*v*. Gloucestershire, 1962
Against Glamorgan	7-33	C. Cook	for Gloucestershire, 1962

Highest Partnerships

For Glamorgan	84	P.M. Walker and W.D. Slade for the 5th wkt *v*. Leicestershire, 1961
Against Glamorgan	105	J.M. Brearley and E.J. Craig for the 1st wkt for Cambridge University, 1963

11
RHOS GROUND, COLWYN BAY

Colwyn Bay CC was founded in 1924, and amongst its early leading lights were the Reverend A.J. Costain, the headmaster of the nearby Rydal School, and various members of the Wooller family. Indeed, it was through the actions of Wilf Wooller that Glamorgan have subsequently travelled up to the North Wales coast to play at the ground which Wilf's father and grandfather helped to establish during the early 1920s in a field off Penrhyn Avenue, near the seafront at Rhos-on-Sea.

The North Wales resort expanded during the inter-war period. Many substantial houses were built near the attractive coastline, and during the summer months Rhos-on-Sea and Old Colwyn attracted many holidaymakers from Lancashire. The Colwyn Bay cricket club also developed a good reputation, and soon secured regular fixtures with clubs in the Manchester and Liverpool area, in addition to visits by touring teams.

During the 1920s the North Wales Cricket Association came into being, and in addition to games with Ireland, Scotland, and the MCC, the new organisation also secured fixtures with the touring teams. The rationale behind these games amongst a heavy schedule for the tourists was to raise money to help boost the game in Wales especially in the North. With the growing popularity of the North Wales resorts, and the likelihood of large crowds of holidaymakers, these matches were staged initially at Llandudno, until 1929, when Rydal School hosted a game between the Wales side and the South Africans. A large crowd turned up and swelled the coffers of the North Wales Association, allowing Denbighshire to enter the Minor County Championship the following year.

1930 also saw Wales play the Minor Counties at the Rhos ground, which Denbighshire also used for their fixtures.

By the outbreak of the Second World War, Colwyn Bay CC had gone from strength to strength, and it had a fully-deserved reputation for being a friendly and competitive club with excellent facilities. During the war, this reputation was further enhanced as the club hosted a number of fund-raising games for the war effort. Amongst the charities to benefit from games at the Rhos-on-Sea ground were the Red Cross Prisoners of War Fund, the Liverpool and Bootle Air Raid Distress Fund, and the Lord Mayor of Manchester's Air Raid Distress Fund.

These wartime friendlies were well attended, and even when hostilities ceased, the ground continued to stage exhibition games. In August 1947, Wilf Wooller brought his Glamorgan side to the Rhos ground to play two-day friendlies against Sir Learie Constantine's XI and a North Wales XI. By the 1950s, this had expanded into a cricket week, with games involving a North Wales representative side, touring teams such as the 1954 Canadians, various Lancashire League XIs, and other scratch teams raised by such individuals as R.W.V. Robins and Vinoo Mankad.

All of these matches boosted further the finances of the Colwyn Bay club and in the 1950s a series of ground improvements were made totalling over £4,000, including an extended pavilion and new dressing rooms. The playing area was also improved, under the watchful eye of groundsman Alf Cassley from 1948 to 1970.

Glamorgan continued to make an annual visit to the ground to play in various exhibition or benefit games. The sizeable crowds and the enhanced facilities by the early 1960s

The seafront at Rhos-on-Sea.

Wilf Wooller – one of the greatest sportsmen produced by Rydal School. He is seen below (sitting on the far right) in the school's XI for 1931. Wooller played regularly for Glamorgan from 1938 until 1960 and was instrumental in bringing county cricket to North Wales.

prompted Wilf Wooller and the other Glamorgan officials to consider whether the Welsh county should stage a first-class fixture at the popular resort. Other seaside towns such as Scarborough, Blackpool and Weston-super-Mare had been staging highly lucrative annual festivals for many years. With fine facilities and a good wicket, plus the prospect of a large crowd of holidaymakers, the county officials felt that it was well worth taking county cricket to the North Wales resort, and they allocated the 1966 Championship match with Derbyshire to the Rhos ground. Their reward was an attendance in excess of 4,000.

Between 1966 and 1974 the Rhos-on-Sea ground staged an annual Championship game or a Sunday League fixture. The match in 1969 with Leicestershire saw a quite remarkable bowling performance by Glamorgan's Tony Cordle. The Barbados-born seam bowler came on as seventh change in the visitors first innings with their score on 86-0. He then dismissed both openers, Maurice Hallam and Mick Norman, in his first three overs, before taking a further seven wickets in a two and a half hour spell, as Leicestershire were dismissed for 203 with Cordle finishing with career-best figures of 24.4-4-49-9.

In April 1973, Yorkshire were the visitors to the Colwyn Bay club, and Geoff Boycott scored an unbeaten 104 in the Sunday League encounter. A record crowd of 2,400 were delighted to see the famous England opener display his batting talents, and gate receipts exceeded £600 – at the time, the second highest in the Rhos club's history. However, Glamorgan had a modest season and, with their income falling and costs rising, a few questions were raised about the viability of taking a match each year to North Wales and

CANADIANS
v
R. W. V. ROBINS XI

CANADIANS
v
R. H MOORE'S XI

COLWYN BAY
v
H. S. BROWN'S XI

WEST INDIES XI
v
C. J. BARNETT'S XI

Colwyn Bay v Warrington

AUSTRALIAN XI
v
S. G. SHEPHERD'S XI

A poster for the 1954 cricket week at Rhos.   *Tony Cordle.*

incurring sizeable expenditure on hotels and mileage for what was, after all, a home game.

In 1972 and 1973, the visits to the Rhos ground were just for Sunday fixtures, but the financial situation did not improve and after the 1974 visit by Sussex, Colwyn Bay was dropped from the county's fixture list. Undeterred, the Colwyn Bay club continued to host Benefit and exhibition games, including, in 1984, the West Indians' match against the League Cricket Conference.

These games continued to be well attended, so when a sponsorship package was offered to the county in 1990 to bring County Championship matches back to the north, the Club's officials decided to allocate the Lancashire match to the Rhos ground, believing it would be attractive to supporters on both sides. It proved to be a massive success, with large crowds for the Championship match and a capacity crowd of 5,000 for the Sunday League fixture. Matthew Maynard, who had been brought up only a few miles away at Menai Bridge, also celebrated by recording Glamorgan's first limited overs century at the ground with a typically explosive innings of 100.

Following the success of the Lancashire game, Colwyn Bay has returned to the club's fixture list, and further ground improvements have taken place, including an extension to the pavilion in 1996. The Glamorgan players and supporters have continued to enjoy their annual visit to North Wales. In the AXA League game in 1993, Adrian Dale took a hat-trick during his spell of 6-22 against Durham, and in the 2000 Championship fixture with Sussex, Steve James established a new club record with 309* – the highest individual innings by a Glamorgan batsman – as the county made 718-3, their highest ever total.

Left: *Adrian Dale – who took a hat-trick at Colwyn Bay in 1993.* Right: *Steve Watkin – who took five wickets for no runs in sixteen balls as Nottinghamshire slumped to 9-6 on the first morning of their game at the Rhos Ground in 1999.*

GROUND STATISTICS FOR COLWYN BAY

First first-class match   *v.* Derbyshire, 27, 28, 29, 30 August 1966

Most recent first-class match   *v.* Lancashire, 1, 2, 3, 4 August 2001

First limited overs match   *v.* Worcestershire, 3 September 1972

Most recent limited overs match   *v.* Lancashire, 5 August 2001

Playing Record

	P	W	L	D	T	Ab/NR
County Championship	14	4	1	9	-	-
First-class friendlies	2	1	-	1	-	-
Sunday League	9	3	5		-	1
National League	3	2	1		-	-

Colwyn Bay.

FIRST-CLASS BATTING RECORDS AT COLWYN BAY

Highest Team Total

| By Glamorgan | 718-3 dec | v. Sussex, 2000 |
| Against Glamorgan | 530 | by Middlesex, 1999 |

Lowest Team Total

| By Glamorgan | 183 | v. Derbyshire, 1966 |
| Against Glamorgan | 118 | by Derbyshire, 1966 |

Highest Individual Score

| By Glamorgan | 309* | S.P. James | v. Sussex, 2000 |
| Against Glamorgan | 155 | M. Watkinson | for Lancashire, 1994 |

Highest Partnership

| By Glamorgan | 377 | by M.T.G. Elliott and S.P. James for the 1st wkt v. Sussex, 2000 |
| Against Glamorgan | 209 | by J.D. Carr and K.R. Brown for the 5th wkt for Middlesex, 1999 |

Steve James.

Mike Watkinson.

BOWLING RECORDS AT COLWYN BAY

Best bowling in an innings in first-class cricket

For Glamorgan	9-49	A.E. Cordle	v. Leicestershire, 1969
Against Glamorgan	7-47	D.C. Morgan	for Derbyshire, 1966

Best bowling in a match in first-class cricket

For Glamorgan	13-110	A.E. Cordle	v. Leicestershire, 1969
Against Glamorgan	9-82	D.C. Morgan	for Derbyshire, 1966

Best bowling in a limited overs match

For Glamorgan	6-22	A. Dale	v. Durham, 1993
Against Glamorgan	4-45	A.R. Oram	for Nottinghamshire, 1997

The groundsman rolling the wicket at Colwyn Bay during one of their successful Festivals in the 1950s.

LIMITED OVERS BATTING RECORDS AT COLWYN BAY

Highest Team Total

By Glamorgan	271-6	*v.* Durham, 1993
Against Glamorgan	246-6	by Lancashire, 1990

Lowest Team Total

By Glamorgan	162-6	*v.* Yorkshire, 1973
Against Glamorgan	105	by Durham, 1993

Highest Individual Score

By Glamorgan	100	M.P. Maynard	*v.* Lancashire, 1990
	100	H. Morris	*v.* Middlesex, 1995
Against Glamorgan	104*	G. Boycott	for Yorkshire, 1973

Highest Partnership

By Glamorgan   143   M.P. Maynard and I.V.A. Richards for the 3rd wkt *v.* Lancs, 1990

Against Glamorgan   129   N.J. Astle and M.P. Dowman for the 4th wkt for Notts, 1997

Matthew Maynard.

Viv Richards.

The photograph above shows the Rhos ground in the mid 1960s, whilst the photograph below shows the pavilion complex from the 1950s, before the improvements and the modern pavilion that resulted in regular county cricket being staged in North Wales.

12

SOPHIA GARDENS, CARDIFF

The history of this tree-lined ground on the west bank of the River Taff, and its name, like so many other features of the Welsh capital city, has a close link with the second Marquess of Bute. The Marquess was the major landowner in Cardiff in the nineteenth century, and he was the man who in 1839 decided to develop the port facilities at the mouth of the Taff. Sophia was the wife of the Marquess, and as the town of Cardiff grew in the middle of the nineteenth century, she became acutely aware that only a limited amount of open space existed in the bustling industrial centre. The only other green area where the townspeople could roam were the Castle Grounds, but they were becoming overcrowded and there were also reports of vandalism.

After seeing many other pleasure gardens elsewhere in the UK and on the Continent, Sophia suggested to the Bute Estate that they should develop the area on the west bank of the river as an attractive area for walking and general recreation, especially for the well-to-do residents of the spacious villas that lined Cathedral Road, the main avenue running north-west from the town centre. Over £1,500 was spent on levelling the ground, planting trees and shrubs, and making broad walkways.

In 1858, the Gardens were formally opened, with the public being allowed access free of charge between the hours of 6 a.m. and 9 p.m. Sadly, in December 1859, Sophia passed away, but by the time of her death, the Gardens had become a huge success, and had taken the pressure off the castle grounds. The Bute Estate therefore decided to further extend the gardens in a northerly direction towards Pontcanna Farm, creating a bowling green, bandstand and a large field for recreation and ball games.

By the late nineteenth century, Sophia Gardens were very popular pleasure grounds where Cardiffians could stroll. The photograph above shows the entrance from Canton Bridge, whilst the photograph below shows the attractive woodland walks and ornamental fountains in the Gardens.

By the end of the century, cricket, football, athletics and cycling were being staged on what had become known as Gala Field, in addition to fêtes, civic galas, horse shows and special events, such as Buffalo Bill's Wild West Show in September 1891, and in June 1899 Barnum and Bailey's travelling circus and menagerie.

After the First World War, Cardiff grew in a northerly direction, and fewer wealthy people lived near the Gardens. No longer was Cardiff a compact town, lying literally in the shadow of the castle. Modern Cardiff now had sprawling suburbs, and the villas in Cathedral Road were no longer the homes of the well-to-do, and were being converted instead into offices and small hotels as their affluent residents moved out to new and spacious homes in the sprawling suburbs to the north, west or east.

Although the number of functions held in the Gardens and on Gala Field had declined, there was still a need for this haven of peace and quiet, less than a mile away from the hustle and bustle of the city's main shopping streets. Consequently, in September 1947 the Fifth Marquis of Bute handed over the whole of the family's estate, including Sophia Gardens, to the City Corporation, on the understanding that they could not build any houses or factories on the Gardens.

Under the terms of their acquisition of land previously owned by the Bute Estate, Cardiff Corporation decided to develop the Castle Grounds into a city centre park and convert Sophia Gardens into a centre for entertainment.

For many years, there had been calls for a venue to hold exhibitions and indoor sporting events, so when they acquired Sophia Gardens, the Corporation decided to convert the large hangar which the RAF had erected in the Gardens, near the Cardiff Bridge entrance, into a pavilion capable of staging musical and theatrical events, as well as exhibitions and conferences.

A postcard from the early 1900s for Sophia Gardens.

The Sophia Gardens Pavilion was formally opened on 27 April 1951. Over the next few years, it played host to many well-known celebrities, including Gracie Fields, Danny Kaye and Cliff Richard, and when Cardiff staged the 1958 Commonwealth Games, the pavilion was used for boxing and wrestling. During the winter of 1982, part of the pavilion's structure collapsed, and the building was demolished. Like much of the southern part of the Gardens, it is now a large car park and only occasionally used by visiting circus troupes.

During the 1950s, various plans were put forward for developing the Gala Field and the adjoining Pontcanna Fields to the north. Plans were submitted for a racecourse, and a multi-purpose recreation complex, including a skating rink, bowling alley and a ballroom. Glamorgan CCC also put in a bid to acquire the Gala Field in order to create a new cricket ground which would help solve the problems caused by the lack of space at Cardiff Arms Park, a mile away to the south.

All of these ideas were initially thrown out, as a faction on the City Council wanted to preserve the Arms Park as the central focus of the city's sporting infrastructure. But the Arms Park was an overcrowded base for the various sections of Cardiff Athletic Club, who saw the Sophia Gardens scheme as a means of moving forward, providing room for further expansion, and creating a National Rugby Stadium in the heart of the Welsh capital.

In 1963, a plan was put forward for the redevelopment of the Arms Park and the acquisition of 23 acres of land at Gala Field, so that the various sections of Cardiff Athletic Club who were losing land at the Arms Park could find a new home. Initially, the plan involved laying out a greyhound track, plus two rugby pitches, tennis courts, and a new cricket pitch, which during the winter months could be used for hockey. However, the greyhound track was dropped from the final draft, which was reduced to just ten and a half acres of Gala Field. In 1964, the City Corporation gave their formal approval, and Cardiff Athletic Club secured a ninety-nine-year lease on the Sophia Gardens area.

During 1965, work began at the former Gala Field, laying out the new wicket, and in August the

following year, Cardiff CC staged their first ever game on the Sophia Gardens wicket, with Cardiff Athletic Reserves playing their counterparts from Newport Athletic Club. Glamorgan also agreed that they would rent the new ground from Cardiff Athletic Club, and stage a minimum of six games a year at Sophia Gardens, providing of course, that a decent wicket was laid out. Building work also began to the south of the new cricket ground creating a large indoor sports centre – now known as the Welsh Institute of Sport.

The move by Cardiff CC from the Arms Park, and the work on creating a new wicket at Sophia Gardens, was all financed by the Welsh Rugby Union. But the building work was not entirely trouble-free, and there were major problems in installing the new drainage system. One of the channels actually ran under the length of the square, parallel with the crease. It caused a ridge to appear midway down the wicket, and rumours started to circulate that the drains had been laid out the wrong way round.

The new dressing room complex, scoreboard and pavilion, built at a cost of £25,000, had all

An aerial view of Sophia Gardens and the pavilion.

been completed by the end of May 1967 when Glamorgan played their inaugural match at the new ground, against the touring Indians. But other sections of the ground were still incomplete, and parts of the ground still looked more like a building site. It was a very damp start to the history of the new ground, as rain washed out the first day's play, and it was not until 3.35 p.m. on the second day that play eventually began, with Sadanand Mohol bowling the first ball to Alan Jones.

Rain continued to interfere with play and, to make matters worse, little of the under cover seating had been completed. It was only after the match with the Indians that the transfer of seating from the Arms Park actually took place, but this was not the end of the teething problems. Although the members had covered enclosures by the time the first Championship match was staged at Sophia Gardens in June 1967, there were complaints about the irregular bounce, and the ridge halfway down the wicket. After several visits by the MCC Inspector of Pitches, remedial work was undertaken by groundsmen Bill Hardiman, Les Sperry, Albert Francis and Richard Stevens. The quality of the square steadily improved, but it was not until the whole square had been relaid during the late 1970s that these problems were finally eradicated.

For several years after their move from the Arms Park, the Glamorgan players and officials were concerned about the unpredictable nature of the new wicket, with batsmen often being struck by sharply rising balls. But this was nothing compared to a near-tragic accident in May 1971, during Glamorgan's match with Warwickshire. This time the wicket had nothing to do whatsoever with events, as Roger Davis, the Glamorgan all-rounder, was hit directly on the temple by a firm legside stroke from Neal Abberley whilst fielding at short leg to the bowling of left-arm seamer Malcolm Nash. These were the days before helmets, and after being struck, Davis collapsed, stopped breathing and went into convulsions. Fortunately, a doctor was sitting in the Members' Enclosure at the River End, and he ran onto the pitch to give Davis the kiss of life. The unfortunate player was taken by ambulance to the Cardiff Infirmary, where he thankfully made a full recovery – but for a few agonising minutes it looked as if Sophia Gardens would enter the history books for all the wrong reasons.

Cardiff CC practice at Sophia Gardens in 1967, with Gordon Eccles, who is still a scoreboard operator at the ground, batting on the newly-laid wicket.

GROUND STATISTICS FOR SOPHIA GARDENS, CARDIFF

First first-class match
v. Indians, 24, 25, 26 May 1967

Most recent first-class match
v. Surrey, 12, 13, 14, 15 September 2001

First limited overs match
v. Somerset, 1 June 1969

Most recent limited overs match
v. Middlesex, 16 September 2001

Playing Record

	P	W	L	D	T	Ab/NR
County Championship	188	38	55	94		1
First-class friendlies	11	1	5	5		-
Gillette/NatWest/C&G	25	15	10		-	-
Benson & Hedges	40	15	22		-	3
Sunday League	96	31	50		-	15
National League	16	13	3		-	-

Sophia Gardens in the mid-1980s.

FIRST-CLASS BATTING RECORDS AT SOPHIA GARDENS, CARDIFF

Highest Team Total

| By Glamorgan | 597-8 dec | *v.* Durham, 1997 |
| Against Glamorgan | 701-9 dec | by Surrey, 2001 |

Lowest Team Total

| By Glamorgan | 31 | *v.* Middlesex, 1997 |
| Against Glamorgan | 52 | by Hampshire, 1968 |

Highest Individual Score

| By Glamorgan | 233* | H. Morris | *v.* Warwickshire, 1997 |
| Against Glamorgan | 313* | S.J. Cook | for Somerset, 1990 |

Highest Partnership

| By Glamorgan | 425* | A. Dale and I.V.A. Richards for the 4th wkt *v.* Middlesex, 1993 |
| Against Glamorgan | 362 | M.D. Moxon and M.P. Vaughan for the 1st wkt for Yorkshire, 1996 |

Viv Richards and Hugh Morris batting against Yorkshire at Cardiff in 1992.

BOWLING RECORDS AT SOPHIA GARDENS, CARDIFF

Best bowling in an innings in first-class cricket

| For Glamorgan | 8-63 | A.W. Allin | v. Sussex, 1976 |
| Against Glamorgan | 9-57 | P.I. Pocock | for Surrey, 1979 |

Best bowling in a match in first-class cricket

| For Glamorgan | 13-127 | R.C. Ontong | v. Nottinghamshire, 1986 |
| Against Glamorgan | 13-102 | D.L. Underwood | for Kent, 1979 |

Best bowling in a limited overs match

For Glamorgan	6-20	R.D.B. Croft	v. Worcestershire, 1994
		S.D. Thomas	v. Comb. Universities, 1995
Against	6-20	T.E. Jesty	for Hampshire, 1975

Rodney Ontong.

Robert Croft.

LIMITED OVERS BATTING RECORDS AT SOPHIA GARDENS, CARDIFF

Highest Team Total

| By Glamorgan | 373-7 | v. Bedfordshire, 1998 |
| Against Glamorgan | 330-4 | by Somerset, 1978 |

Lowest Team Total

| By Glamorgan | 86 | v. Warwickshire, 1995 |
| Against | 69 | by Hampshire, 2000 |

Highest Individual Score

| By Glamorgan | 154* | H. Morris | v. Staffordshire, 1989 |
| Against | 145 | P.W. Denning | for Somerset, 1978 |

Highest Partnership

By Glamorgan   192* S.P. James and H. Morris for the 1st wkt v. Dorset, 1995
Against Glamorgan   213   M.D. Moxon and A.A. Metcalfe for the 1st wkt for Yorkshire, 1991

The visit of HRH Prince Charles and Diana, Princess of Wales, to the Sophia Gardens ground in 1987.

On 5 September 1969, Glamorgan defeated Worcestershire by 147 runs to win the County Championship for the second time. Their victory was set up by a magnificent innings from Majid Khan, with the Pakistani looking completely at ease on a wicket of quite variable bounce. Despite the loss of partners at regular intervals, Majid scored 114* before lunch and completely dominated the bowling in an innings which many still consider the finest to have been played at the ground.

Sophia Gardens was also the scene of a record-breaking partnership of 425 – the highest for any wicket by Glamorgan batsmen – between Viv Richards and Adrian Dale in the 1993 Championship match with Middlesex. It was also the venue of the famous Sunday League match in September 1976 when Somerset arrived in Cardiff, needing to beat Glamorgan to secure their first ever title. Given the Welsh county's poor form and lowly standing in the League, it seemed a mere formality. However, it was a far more evenly fought contest than many thought, and it culminated in a pulsating finish, with Graham Burgess run out off the final ball to leave Glamorgan the victors by one run.

Wilf Wooller once described Sophia Gardens as having 'a quite delightful rural setting, spacious and well-treed, but somehow it has never reproduced the cosy atmosphere of Cardiff Arms Park, with more than a century of traditional sporting activity.' This cosiness has now disappeared following the purchase of the ground by Glamorgan in the winter of 1995/96, and the start of an ambitious development plan costing £9 million.

Work began in the winter of 1998/99 after the club secured £2.8 million of lottery funding, and already a new administration block has been completed, together with sponsors' boxes and dining facilities, plus a lavish new Indoor School, with start-of-the-art facilities and seven lanes of indoor nets. New seating has also been erected at the river end of the ground, plus a new scoreboard facility – all in time for the 1999 World Cup, which saw the Welsh county host the Australian squad, and stage their zonal match against New Zealand. The success of this match, and the other ground improvements, led to Sophia Gardens staging the One Day International between Pakistan and Australia in June 2001, and in 2002 the England side will stage a one-day game against a Welsh side.

New outdoor nets and training areas have also been laid out as the Cardiff ground has been transformed into an impressive Centre of Excellence for cricket in Wales. The county club have also created their own academy based at the ground, under the directorship of Steve Watkin, the former Glamorgan stalwart. Over the next few years, further ground improvements will take place with a new Pavilion at the Cathedral Road end of the ground, a media centre, further covered seating for spectators and more sponsors' boxes, as an 8,000-seater stadium takes shape and a top-class venue, worthy of a capital city.

Floodlit cricket comes to Cardiff.

13

B.P. LLANDARCY

In 1921, National Oil Refineries Ltd built a refinery at Llandarcy, a small village some two miles south-west of Neath, close to the mouth of the River Neath on the Bristol Channel. The company also acquired an area of adjoining farmland upon which they provided recreational facilities for their employees. Amongst the facilities provided was a cricket club, and during the 1930s the company (later to be taken over by British Petroleum) oversaw ground improvements, the construction of changing rooms and a pavilion, as well as the creation of a decent wicket.

The reputation of the Llandarcy wicket had grown sufficiently by the late 1940s for Glamorgan to consider it for some of their second team games. After a visit in May 1949 by the county's Club and Ground XI against the B.P. club, the ground was allocated the Minor County fixture with Gloucestershire Second XI in 1950. Rain interrupted play, but the Glamorgan officials were suitably impressed with the Llandarcy facilities, and it continued to host Second XI matches, as well as Glamorgan's two-day match against the Pakistani Eaglets in 1958.

By this time, Len Pitchford, the former Glamorgan batsman, was acting as the groundsman, and under his supervision, further improvents took place to the wicket. His efforts were rewarded in 1971 as the ground was allocated Glamorgan's match on 7, 8 and 9 July against Oxford University, as part of the fiftieth anniversary celebrations at the refinery complex.

Glamorgan 299 (R.C. Fredericks 94, K.J. Lyons 53, M. St J. Burton 3-54) and 133 (A.R. Wingfield-Digby 3-24, M. St J. Burton 4-45)

Oxford University 204 (B. May 38, D.L. Williams 4-43, M.J. Llewellyn 3-30) and 182 (G.A. Robinson 62, P.M. Walker 3-42)

Llandarcy has not staged any further first-class matches, but until 1992, it continued to host Second XI games. During the late 1980s, it was also used as the home venue for the Glamorgan Colts side, who participated in the South Wales Cricket Association.

Roy Fredericks.

Lawrence Williams.

14
PEN-Y-POUND, ABERGAVENNY

Abergavenny is widely regarded to be one of the most picturesque grounds on the first-class circuit. The intimate atmosphere and rural location, nestling amongst the tree-topped hills on the Welsh border, a mile or so to the north of a small and friendly market town, plus its quaint pavilion and irregular boundary, all provide a timely reminder of what cricket must have been like in the pre-commercial era.

The Abergavenny club dates back to 1834, and since 1896 they have been playing at the Avenue Road ground on land owned by the Marquess of Abergavenny. The Marquess proved to be a kind benefactor to the cricket club, financing the building of the pavilion and covering the costs of creating a decent wicket. The reward for all this effort was the addition of Abergavenny to the Monmouthshire fixture list, and in 1910 the Avenue Road ground staged their Minor County fixture with Carmarthenshire.

In 1935, Glamorgan merged with Monmouthshire in 1935, and Second XI plus club and ground fixtures subsequently took place at Abergavenny. In 1948, the ground hosted Glamorgan's Minor County fixture with Devon, and with Glamorgan pledging to stage first-class matches in Monmouthshire, the Abergavenny officials hoped that their attractive home would soon host a Championship fixture.

However, the superior facilities and larger pavilion at Ebbw Vale won the day, and Abergavenny continued to stage just second team and benefit matches. But a series of ground improvements occurred after a fire in 1977 had severely damaged the pavilion and completely destroyed the adjoining tea-room. A generous grant from the Welsh Sports Council helped to pay for the renovations and the creation of much larger facilities, and all at a time when Glamorgan were staging more games at out-grounds.

The Abergavenny club duly made a request to stage a Sunday League game, and in 1981 they were allocated the match with neighbours Worcestershire, followed in 1982 by the fixture with Northamptonshire. The Glamorgan officials were suitably impressed by the hard work, both on and off the field by the Abergavenny folk, as well as the generous sponsorship from local businesses, so in May 1983 the Abergavenny ground staged its inaugural County Championship fixture.

Worcestershire and Gloucestershire have been regular vistors to Avenue Road, and their batsmen, as well as the Glamorgan players, have taken full advantage of the placid wicket and small boundaries. One of the best examples was the 1990 fixture against Worcestershire, as Graeme Hick recorded a superb 252*. Phil Neale, the visiting captain, then set Glamorgan a target of 495 to win on the final day, and the Welsh side ended on 493-6, and came agonisingly close to setting a new Championship record.

However, the most famous game in the ground's short Championship history came in August 1995, as Andrew Symonds made 254 and smashed the world record for the most number of sixes in a first-class match. The Australian hit 16 in his double-century, followed by four more in the second innings. Almost unnoticed, Indian all-rounder Javagal Srinath, claimed 13-150, and his supreme efforts, on a ground regarded as a bowler's graveyard, were in keeping with the almost unreal atmosphere which is generated by this most idiosyncratic, and charming, of county cricket venues.

Andrew Symonds relaxes after his record-breaking innings for Gloucestershire at Abergavenny in 1995, which contained 16 sixes.

GROUND STATISTICS FOR ABERGAVENNY

First first-class match   *v.* Worcestershire, 22, 23, 24 June 1983

Most recent first-class match   *v.* Northamptonshire, 20, 21, 22, 23 August 1997

Playing Record

	P	W	L	D
County Championship	14	3	3	8
Sunday League	2	1	1	

The details of the two limited overs games staged at Abergavenny were:

10 May 1981

> Worcestershire 170-7 (E.J.O. Hemsley 43, M.A. Nash 2-31) beat
> Glamorgan 152 (R.C. Ontong 30, J. Birkenshaw 3-17) by 18 runs

5 September 1982

> Glamorgan 229-7 (R.C. Ontong 100, D.J. Capel 2-39) beat
> Northamptonshire 153-7 (R.G. Williams 42, M.A. Nash 2-21)
> on a faster scoring rate

A view of the Abergavenny ground from the pavilion dining room.

FIRST-CLASS BATTING RECORDS AT ABERGAVENNY

Highest Team Total

By Glamorgan	514-9 dec	v. Gloucestershire, 1991
Against Glamorgan	514-4 dec	by Worcestershire, 1990

Lowest Team Total

By Glamorgan	168	v. Derbyshire, 1986
Against Glamorgan	140	by Gloucestershire, 1991

Highest Individual Score

By Glamorgan	164	M.P. Maynard	v. Gloucestershire, 1995
Against Glamorgan	254*	A. Symonds	for Gloucestershire, 1995

Highest Partnership

By Glamorgan	306	M.P. Maynard and D.L. Hemp for the 3rd wkt v. Gloucestershire, 1995
Against Glamorgan	264	G.A. Hick and D.B. D'Oliveira for the 3rd wkt for Worcestershire, 1990

David Hemp.

Matthew Maynard.

BOWLING RECORDS AT ABERGAVENNY

Best bowling in an innings in first-class cricket

For Glamorgan	6-56	Waqar Younis	v. Northamptonshire, 1997
Against Glamorgan	9-76	J. Srinath	for Gloucestershire, 1996

Best bowling in a match in first-class cricket

For Glamorgan	10-134	Waqar Younis	v. Northamptonshire, 1997
Against Glamorgan	13-150	J. Srinath	for Gloucestershire, 1995

Left: *Malcolm Nash – the Abergavenny-born player who led Glamorgan in 1980 and 1981.*
Right: *Waqar Younis.*

Abergavenny CC with members of the Glamorgan team who played the club in a friendly in 1938.

Alan Butcher batting at Abergavenny in 1990.

15

HOOVERS SPORTS GROUND, MERTHYR TYDFIL

In the early nineteenth century, Merthyr Tydfil was the largest industrial settlement in South Wales, and the bustling town boasted four huge ironworks – Dowlais, Cyfarthfa, Plymouth and Penydarren. By 1823, these were producing forty-three per cent of Britain's iron and the works attracted hundreds of migrants. A formal cricket club was created in 1831, but few others developed, as the steelworkers had long hours of work, with many being of quite humble means and unable to afford the subscription fees.

In the 1850s, these barriers were broken down by the benevolent attitude of the wealthy ironmasters, who were eager to improve the quality of life of their employees. In 1852, the Guest family gave access to a field for their staff at the Dowlais works, whilst in 1857 the Crawshay family who owned the Cyfarthfa Works followed suit. The spread of Muscular Christianity led to the formation of other teams in the second half of the twentieth century, with the Hills Plymouth team emerging as one of the most successful in the region.

Steel-making in the valleys of South Wales started to decline in the early twentieth century, and as the steelworks closed and people drifted away, so the cricket teams diminuished.

Football, rugby and boxing all grew in popularity, but after the Second World War, cricket in Merthyr was boosted by the arrival of light industry, and in particular, one company – the Hoover Electrical Company, who, on 1 March 1948, opened a new factory to the south of Merthyr at Pentrebach, making washing machines and tumble dryers.

The opening of the Hoovers factory created over 2,000 jobs, and like the earlier ironmasters, Hoovers decided to create a recreational complex for their many employees. Alongside the factory was an area of railway sidings, which following the closure of the mines and steel foundries were now in a semi-derelict state. The company bought the land, reclaimed and levelled it, and so created the Hoovers Sports Ground.

By 1953, the wicket was ready for competitive matches, and in June Wilf Wooller led a Glamorgan Club and Ground XI against a combined Hoover and Merthyr XI. Over the next few years, regular benefit matches were staged at the ground, together with a fixture involving the 1957 Pakistan Eaglets. It had always been the dream of the Hoover's management that their sports ground would stage county matches. In the 1980s their dreams came true, as together with the local council and other businesses, they put together a sponsorship deal that led to Glamorgan playing Sunday League Cricket at Merthyr in 1988 and 1989.

5 June 1988   Glamorgan 134 (A.R. Butcher 34, C.S. Cowdrey 4-20) lost to Kent 135-5 (N.R. Taylor 62) by 5 wickets

11 June 1989   Glamorgan 209-6 (R.J. Shastri 92) beat Middlesex 172 (J.D. Carr 41, R.J. Shastri 3-33, R.C. Ontong 3-32) by 37 runs

Although no further Sunday League games have been staged at the Hoovers Sports Ground, the ground has continued to host stage Second XI matches, in addition to some of the Wales Minor Counties fixtures.

Ravi Shastri.

Rodney Ontong.

116

16
THE OVAL, LLANDUDNO

Cricket was first played in Llandudno during the 1850s, and in August 1866 when the United All England Eleven played a XXII of Conwy and District, the home side included players from the Llandudno area. In 1890, Llandudno CC was formed, and the following year they held a cricket week, which included a match against an MCC side. The following year, the cricket week included a match between a North Wales XI and the MCC.

Llandudno CC have played at a ground in Gloddaeth Avenue since 1891, just half a mile away from the pretty seafront and the famous promentary called the Great and Little Orme. Their ground, known as The Oval, was laid out on land they leased from the Mostyn Family of Gloddaeth Hall. The Hon. Henry Mostyn was captain of the club at the time, and he and his family did much to develop and popularise the North Wales resort.

After the First World War, various ground improvements were made, including a pavilion, which was opened on 8 September 1924 by Lord Mostyn before the start of a two-day game between the touring South Africans and a North Wales XI. Indeed, the developments at The Oval were part of an attempt by Mostyn and his supporters in the North Wales Cricket Association to bring first-class cricket to an annual cricket festival on the North Wales coast, and to create a Welsh team.

In May 1923, a match was staged at the ground between North Wales and South Wales, following the creation of the Welsh Cricket Union. This saw a merger between the interests of Glamorgan and the professional organisations in South Wales with the North Wales Cricket Association, and the result was a series of first-class matches involving a Welsh side. Their game against the Gentlemen of Ireland became the inaugural first-class contest at Llandudno in 1925, with Wales winning a very one-sided affair by an innings. However, the success further fuelled the ambition of the North Wales Association, and in 1927 the New Zealand tourists visited The Oval for matches against Wales and The Cygnets. The latter were an all-Welsh amateur XI, who included Norman Riches and Maurice Turnbull of Glamorgan, plus Lord Aberdare, alias the Hon. C.N. Bruce of Middlesex.

1928 saw The Gentlemen of Ireland return to Llandudno, together with the West Indians who were beaten by 8 wickets by the Welsh side thanks to a sterling bowling performance by Sidney Barnes. The former England bowler was living in nearby Colwyn Bay, and the fifty-two year old showed that he had not lost any of his wiles, taking 7-51 and 5-67. Also in the Welsh side that defeated the 1928 West Indians were Donald Boumphrey and Alan Ratcliffe – a housemaster and pupil respectively from Rydal School, the public school in Colwyn Bay – and Ratcliffe, in front of many of his friends the school, occupied the crease for over two hours in making a composed half-century.

His success and the emergence of Rydal as a sporting centre, resulted in the school staging Wales' match with the 1929 South Africans, whilst in 1930 Wales' games were allocated to Colwyn Bay club in nearby Rhos-on-Sea. Lancashire and various teams from the Northern Leagues continued to visit the Llandudno Oval for special exhibition matches and friendlies, but no more first-class matches were staged in Llandudno, and the club disbanded during the Second World War.

In 1949, The Oval was purchased by the Llandudno Urban District Council, and in 1950 the Llandudno club reformed. Once again, it hosted various benefit and exhibition games during the holiday season, and the success of these and the county games at nearby Rhos-on-Sea led Glamorgan to stage a Sunday League fixture at The Oval on 22 June 1969.

Leicestershire 141-8 (B.R. Knight 39, R. Illingworth 31, D.L. Williams 2-26, Majid Khan 2-26) lost to Glamorgan 74–0 (B.A. Davis 29*, A. Jones 32*) by ten wickets

Disaster hit the club in 1973 when fire destroyed the pavilion. It was subsequently rebuilt and in 1978 the ground hosted an exhibition match between a North Wales Invitation XI and the Pakistan International Airways side. However, Glamorgan have not returned for any more county games.

An aerial view of Llandudno from the Great Orme.

17

PARC-Y-DWRLYN, PENTYRCH

Pentyrch is a dormitory settlement, some eight miles north-west of the centre of Cardiff. Until the 1950s, Pentyrch was a typical small village, but it has expanded recently, with its pleasant setting on the rural fringes of the Welsh capital making it very popular with commuters who work in Cardiff.

In 1993, Glamorgan played one Sunday League match at the Parc-y-Dwrlyn ground in Pentyrch. The ground is the home of the Pentyrch and Old Monktonians CC, who at the time played in the Glamorgan and Gwent Conference.

The club was created in the 1880s by the former pupils of Monkton House School, Cardiff's oldest boys' grammar school, which occupied a site to the east of the city centre, adjacent to the well-to-do suburb of Tredegarville. The old boys were eager to create a cricket and rugby club, in order to maintain friendships and sporting activity, and so successful were they that their rugby team evolved into Glamorgan Wanderers RFC in 1913.

The Old Monktonians CC continued to be a successful team in the Cardiff and District Leagues, playing at various grounds in the suburbs of Cardiff. By the 1980s, 'The Old Monks' wanted a permanent home, and in 1983 they secured one in the village of Pentyrch, sharing the Parc-y-Dwrlyn recreation ground with Pentyrch RFC. A close relationship has subsequently evolved between the cricket club and the local residents, and in 1990 the club's name was amended to include that of the village. This amalgamation was followed by a number of significant improvements, including extensions to the pavilion in 1991, and the construction of a new scorebox in 1992.

Glamorgan's visit to Pentyrch in 1993 was the result of an agreement between the county club and Taff-Ely Borough Council to stage an annual match within the authority's boundaries. Glamorgan had been staging games at Pontypridd, but after experiencing parking difficulties at Ynysangharad Park, the 1993 AXA League fixture with Northamptonshire was allocated to Pentyrch, despite the fact that the club had not even played a Second XI match at the ground!

May 23, 1993   Glamorgan 169-9 (A. Dale 43, J.P. Taylor 3-32, N.G.B. Cook 4-22) lost to
                      Northamptonshire 170-7 (R.J. Bailey 49, D.J. Capel 47, S.L. Watkin 2-28) by 3 wickets

Significant improvements have subsequently been made to the Pontypridd ground, and the 1993 fixture against Northamptonshire remains Glamorgan's only ever visit to Parc-y-Dwrlyn. In 2001, the Pentyrch club joined the newly-formed Thomas Carroll South Wales Premier League, and won the competition.

A photograph of the pretty village of Pentyrch in the early 1920s.

18

VICARAGE FIELD, ABERYSTWYTH

On two occasions, Glamorgan have played Sunday League games at Vicarage Field, which forms part of the sports complex owned by the University College of Wales in Aberystwyth. The ground takes its name from the vicarage associated with Llanbadarn Church, and forms part of an area leased to the University by David Davies of Llandinam in 1906.

The field was levelled and subsequently used for athletics, soccer, rugby and cricket. In the years either side of the First World War, changing rooms and a pavilion were erected at Vicarage Field. Glamorgan used the university's facilities for the pre-season training during the 1930s, and after the Second World War, the county sent a team to Aberystwyth for an annual game either against the University or a combined Welsh Universities XI.

On 31 July 1977, the ground staged their Sunday League match with Essex at the University's ground as part of the town's 900th Centenary celebrations. It ended in a 15-run victory for the visitors:

Essex 234-7 (G.A. Gooch 80, K.W.R. Fletcher 46, G. Richards 3-42)
Glamorgan 219-7 (C.L. King 66, J.A. Hopkins 40, G.A. Gooch 2-28)

On 27 August 1989, the county revisited the Aberystwyth ground as part of their Centenary celebrations for their Sunday League match with Warwickshire. Once again, though, the game ended in defeat for Glamorgan, this time by 6 wickets:

Glamorgan 203-4 (H. Morris 83, I. Smith 56*)
Warwickshire 207-4 (T.A. Lloyd 56*, D.A. Reeve 56*)

Cricket in Aberystwyth can be traced back to 1830. The club played at Gogerddan, the home of Pryse Pryse, the local MP. However, the club's activities largely consisted of practices and single wicket contests between club members. Aberystwyth was at the time a twelve-hour stage coach ride from Carmarthen, and to make matters worse the service only ran on Tuesdays, Thursdays and Saturdays. The opening of a railway line to Aberystwyth helped to overcome this barrier, and in July 1869 Llanelly CC hired a special excursion train for their match against the Ceredigion club at Aberystwyth.

The University College of Wales Aberystwyth cricket XI of 1909.

19

CHRIST COLLEGE, BRECON

During the 1990s, Christ College, Brecon hosted two one-day games – one involved Glamorgan and the other Wales, but both were against touring teams – the 1991 West Indians and the 1993 Zimbabweans.

Cricket at the public school began during the 1850s and their fixture list soon included games with top grammar schools in South Wales, as well as from 1865 Llandovery College, the other leading public school in South Wales. The growth of cricket at Christ College was due to the actions of the Revd M.A. Farrar, who introduced cricket as the first team sport at the school. In 1857, Christ College rented a field in the town for cricket, and the following year, Farrar was able to organise matches against Brecon United Morning Club, as well as the Brecon Town side in 1859.

By 1880, the school were sufficiently strong to enter the South Wales Challenge Cup, and to the young scholars' delight, they progressed to the semi-final of the prestigious competition, before losing to Cardiff CC by one run in a most nail-biting encounter.

By this time the headmaster was Revd D.L. Lloyd, and over the course of the next few years, he and his staff gave further encouragement to the talented young players in their charge. Also on the staff were two Oxford graduates – A.J. Tuckwell, a forceful opening bat, and W.S. Rawson, a soccer blue and England footballer, who had played Minor County cricket for Herefordshire.

Several Breconians subsequently went on to play for Glamorgan in county cricket, including in 1890, Robert Ajax Lewis, a left-handed batsman and spin bowler, who scored an accomplished 52 against Somerset at Bath, and took 3-9 against Gloucestershire at Bristol in 1891. Dr Teddy Morgan, who had been in the college team in the 1890s, played for Glamorgan against Devon at Exeter in 1903 , the year after making his debut on the wing for the Welsh rugby team. His county cricket career was brief, but Teddy went into Welsh sporting history after scoring a try in Wales' famous victory over the New Zealand All Blacks in 1905.

Guy Morgan was another talented all-round sportsman from Christ College, who played in 45 matches for Glamorgan between 1925 and 1938, as well as playing cricket and rugby for both Cambridge University and Wales. In all, Guy won 8 Welsh caps, and also appeared for Swansea, London Welsh and the Barbarians. On the cricket field, his finest hour came at Horsham in 1929, where an aggressive innings of 91* helped Glamorgan recover after following-on, and they eventually defeated Sussex in a quite remarkable Championship match.

The success of tourist matches at Neath showed how promoting sport could boost the local economy, and as a result several organisations also considered hosting flag-flying matches in other locations. The Development Board for Rural Wales were instrumental in organising the 55-overs friendly on 15 July 1991 between Wales Minor Counties and the West Indian tourists. The visitors, led by Viv Richards, strolled to a comfortable victory with Carl Hooper hitting 88 off 43 balls, whilst Brian Lara made 82, Phil Simmons 64 and Richards 68.

On 5 September 1993, the Zimbabweans were the visitors to Christ College for a 55-overs match against Glamorgan.

> Glamorgan 221-8 (S.P. James 77, U. Ranchod 3-34) beat
> Zimbabwe 168 (A.D.R. Campbell 43, R.P. Lefebvre 2-18) by 53 runs

Although they have not returned for any more first team games, Glamorgan have also staged Second XI matches at Christ College against Somerset in 1996 and Hampshire in 1997.

The Christ College Brecon cricket XI of 1905.

20

BARRY

Barry Athletic Cricket Club's ground at Barry Island, some nine miles south-west of Cardiff, staged a number of friendly games both during and after the Second World War. A nomadic club had been formed in Barry in the late nineteenth century, and in 1904 they acquired an area of land, close to the seafront, from the Jenner family of Wenvoe Castle, and developed their own ground.

The Barry club expanded in the inter-war period, with Ronnie Boon, Harold Dickinson and Frank Pinch going on to win places in the Glamorgan side. By the early 1930s, the Barry Athletic Club had become one of the leading clubs in the region and, given their excellent wicket, Glamorgan duly staged Club and ground games at the Island ground. These were followed in 1936 and 1937 by Minor County Championship matches against Berkshire, as well as the two-day friendly with the Phoenix Club of Ireland in 1938.

With the Arms Park and St Helen's being used by the military authorities, Barry staged a number of special exhibition and fund-raising contests during the Second World War. These included games in 1943 against the Anti-Aircraft Command and the RAF, followed in 1944 by matches against Learie Constantine's XI and the West of England. In 1945, Learie Constantine's XI were the visitors again, and when county cricket resumed in the late 1940s, the ground continued to stage Second XI and Minor County fixtures, with the opponents including Lancashire Second XI, Devon and Middlesex Second XI.

The success of these matches, and the decent attendances from visiting holidaymakers led to

Glamorgan allocating their two-day friendly against the RAF on 12 and 13 July 1950 to the Barry ground.

Glamorgan 245 (S.W. Montgomery 84, D.R. Davies 35, A. Wainwright 3-47) and 25-0
RAF 137 (W. Fisk 42*, J.E. McConnon 7-33) and 180 (A.C. Shirreff 56, J.E. McConnon 4-23)

The game resulted in a draw, and afterwards, the Barry club hoped they might be allocated a Championship fixture. But the absence of permanent seating meant that Glamorgan's visits were subsequently restricted to Second XI fixtures.

An aerial view of the seafront at Barry Island, with part of the cricket ground on the extreme left.

21
CARDIFF BARRACKS GROUND

Many people believe that Glamorgan have only played on two grounds in Cardiff – at the Arms Park and Sophia Gardens. But in fact, during the immediate post-war period they also staged games at the Barracks ground at Maindy, two miles to the north of the city centre.

The Barracks were opened in 1876 and the military authorities laid out a sports field to the west of the camp so that the camp's personnel could partake in healthy recreation. The ground was first used by Glamorgan in August 1945 for a one-day game between a Glamorgan Past XI and a Glamorgan Future XI. Both the Arms Park and the St Helen's ground in Swansea were unavailable, so when the military authorities offered the use of the Barracks Field for the game, the Glamorgan committee accepted their offer.

The wicket proved to be a good one, so with Glamorgan considering a suitable venue for their Service games in the late 1940s, the two-day friendly match against the RAF on 3 and 4 August 1949 was allocated to the Barracks Ground.

> Glamorgan 233 (M. Robinson 73, R.G. Wilson 4-60) and 190-8 dec (W. Wooller 50, W.G.A. Parkhouse 42, W. Greensmith 4-43) beat
> RAF. 108 (W. Greensmith 33, B.L. Muncer 4-27, J.S. Pressdee 4-37) and 42 (B.L. Muncer 6-14) by 273 runs

During the 1950s, the ground was used again for club and ground matches as well as the match with Gloucestershire Second XI in 1952. During the 1950s, the city of Cardiff expanded in a northerly direction, and with the end of National Service, the Barracks were scaled down. Consequently, the land at Maindy became attractive for building development and the military authorities began to dispose of the land. In 1966, the cricket field was sold and it is now occupied by Companies House.

An aerial view of the Maindy Stadium complex in the 1950s, with the Barracks Ground in the top left-hand corner.